Media Law in Spain

Media Law in Spain

Ana Azurmendi
Carles Llorens

This book was originally published as a monograph in the International Encyclopaedia of Laws/Media Law.

Founding Editor: Roger Blanpain
General Editor: Frank Hendrickx
Volume Editors: Peggy Valcke & Eva Lievens

Wolters Kluwer

Published by:
Kluwer Law International B.V.
PO Box 316
2400 AH Alphen aan den Rijn
The Netherlands
E-mail: international-sales@wolterskluwer.com
Website: lrus.wolterskluwer.com

Sold and distributed in North, Central and South America by:
Wolters Kluwer Legal & Regulatory U.S.
7201 McKinney Circle
Frederick, MD 21704
United States of America
Email: customer.service@wolterskluwer.com

Sold and distributed in all other countries by:
Air Business Subscriptions
Rockwood House
Haywards Heath
West Sussex
RH16 3DH
United Kingdom
Email: international-customerservice@wolterskluwer.com

Printed on acid-free paper

ISBN 978-94-035-0310-3

e-Book: ISBN 978-94-035-0191-8
web-PDF: ISBN 978-94-035-0250-2

Printed in the United Kingdom.

The Authors

Ana Azurmendi is a Graduate in Law and in Journalism. She has PhD from the University of Navarra, Spain. She is professor of Media Law at the Faculty of Communication since 1991 and Director of the Center for Internet Studies and Digital Life, University of Navarra. She has participated in political and institutional projects as an expert: in the Commission on the Project of Reform of Basque Broadcasting, Basque Parliament (December 2016), in the Commission on the New Audiovisual Law of Galicia, Galician Parliament (December 2010) and in the Commission on the Right of Reply, Mexican Senate (January 2014). She was also a Consultant of the Legal Vice-presidency, Televisa Corporation, on the issues Pluralism and Cross-ownership, Must-Carry and Must-Offer Duties and Right of Reply in Mexico (October 2013).

She was appointed as professor at the 'Comparative Media Law' Programme, University of Oxford (summer 2006) and at University of Paris II (spring 2003); at the Doctoral Programme on 'Human Rights', University of Salamanca and Panamericana University (2007–2008) in México DF; at the Doctoral Programme on 'Media Law' of UNAM-University of Occidente-Iberoamericana University (2000–2003), in Michoacán, Sinaloa, México. She has been the professor of Intellectual Property at the Master on 'Digital Creativity and Communication', University of Coruña, Spain (1998–2009). She is leading the I+D Research Project: *Transformation on the Regional Television* (2013–2017) sponsored by the Ministry of Economy of Competitiveness. She has been a researcher of different projects: PIUNA Project *The Impact of digitization on the Audiovisual Industry in Spain* (2010–2013); I+D Project, sponsored by the Ministry of Science and Innovation: *Internet impact to the redefinition of the Spanish Regional Public Broadcasting* (2009–2012). She has been the leader of the I+D project: *Public Broadcasting The Challenge of the Digital Era* (2004–2007) sponsored by the Ministry of Education and Science, and of the Contract of Research on *Audiovisual Authorities* with the Audiovisual Authority of Navarra (2008). Editor of the Spanish journal *Communication&Society* (1997–2013).She has been a visiting professor at the Silha

The Authors

Center for the Study of Media Ethics and Law de la University of Minnesota, USA in 1993, at the Faculty of Administrative Studies, University of York, Toronto, Canada in 1995, at the Center for Socio-Legal Studies de la Universidad de Oxford, UK in 2006 and 2007, at the Department of Politics, University of Manchester, UK in 2011 and at the School of Journalism University of North Carolina, USA in 2013.
She is the author of books *Derecho de la Comunicación* (2016 and 2011), *La Reforma de la Televisión Pública Española* (2007), *El derecho a la propia imagen* (1997 and 1998), *El Consejo Audiovisual de Navarra. Sus funciones y competencias en el contexto europeo de regulación del sector audiovisual* (2009) among others.
Her books have been cited in the case law on freedom of expression by the Constitutional Court of Chile and Peru and by the Parliamentary Commission on regulation of the rights of journalists in Mexico.

Carles Llorens holds an MA in Communication Science (1992) from the Autonomous University of Barcelona, Spain and a Ph Din Audiovisual Communication from the same University (2001) for his 'thesis*European Media Concentration and Pluralism: The European Union Action' (Spanish)*.He is associate professor at the Communication Faculty of the Autonomous University of Barcelona since 2003. He was the coordinator of Audiovisual Communication undergraduate degree at the same faculty (2010–2013) and Associate Dean since 2013. The main lines of his research are European and Spanish media concentration issues, Catalan Radio and European Media Policy. Member of research group GRISS since 1998 and scientific partner at INCOM since 2005. Both research centres are located at the Autonomous University of Barcelona. He was an academic visitor at Oxford University, at the Center for Socio Legal-Studies from March 2006 to February 2007. He was awarded a Marie Curie Fellowship from 1996 to 1998 at the CRID (Centre de Recherches Informatique et Droit). Namur University, Belgium. His research project was to study the telecommunications and broadcasting convergence. He has been a member of COST A30 action: 'East of West: Setting a New Central Eastern European Media Research Agenda' (2006–2009).He worked as a journalist from 1993 to 1996 at news agency *Europa Press* and at sport newspaper *Marca* and he worked as a producer at 'Onda Cero-Onda Rambla' FM radio. He is the member of the ULEPICC España (Union Latina de Economía Política de la Información, la Comunicación y la Cultura), ECREA (European Communication

Research and Education Association), thematic section 'Communication Law and Policy' and EMMA (European Media Management Education Association).

The Authors

Table of Contents

Table of Contents

List of Abbreviations

AEDE	Asociación Española de Editores
CCMA	Corporació Catalana de Mitjans Audiovisuals
CEMA	Consejo Estatal de Medios Audiovisuales
CETV	Corporación Extremadura Televisión
CIS	Centro de Investigaciones Sociológicas
CNMC	Comisión Nacional del Mercado y la Competencia /The National Markets and Competition Commission
CMTV	Castilla-La Mancha Televisión
CRTVG	Corporación de Radio e Television
DDT	Digital Decoder Television
DTT / TDT	Digital Terrestrial Television /Televisión Digital Terrestre
EITB	Euskal Irrati Telebista
EU	European Union
FAPE	Federación de Asociaciones de Periodistas Españoles
FDF	Factoría de Ficción. Fiction Factory. An A3 Media Channel specialized on Fiction.
FORTA	Federación de los Organismos de Televisión Autonómica /Regional Broadcasting Corporations Association
IPTV	Internet Protocol Television
RTVE	Radio Televisión Española
RTVC	Radio Televisión Canarias
RNE	Radio Nacional Española
PATV	Principado de Asturias Televisión
RTRM	Radio Televisión Región de Murcia
STC	Sentencia del Tribunal Constitucional
TVE	Televisión Española
VOD	Video on Demand

General Introduction

§1. General Background of the Country

A. Political and Legal System of the Country

1. Spain is a young democracy, achieved after a very difficult but successful political period of transition, which followed the end of Franco's dictatorship in 1975. It is a constitutional monarchy with the structure of an autonomous state, composed of seventeen autonomous regions, plus two autonomous cities Ceuta and Melilla, in Africa.

B. Geography and Population

2. The population of Spain is estimated at 46,524,943 (INE Padrón: 2016). Due to the economic crisis, during the last five years, the phenomenon of immigration from Latin America, Africa and East-Europe has been stabilizing after years of exponential increase. These new minorities represent 9.8% of the population (INE Padrón: 2016). In fact, they have transformed the dynamics of many cities and villages throughout Spain.

3. Some regions have a strong political, social and cultural identity like the Basque Country, Catalonia and Galicia. The three of these have their own languages: Basque, Catalan and Gallego. Especially in the case of the Basque Country and Catalonia, the separatist movements are very active. In 2011, the Basque terrorist group ETA declared a permanent ceasefire, after more than fifty years of violence. In the case of Catalonia, the more representatively pro-independence action was the consultation of 2017 of the independence of Catalonia. It was organized by the Catalonian government with the support of the Catalonian Parliament, but it was prohibited by the central government with the support of the State General Prosecutor. Finally, the consultation was celebrated on 1 October 2017, in an atmosphere of political tension and police repression; but it was considered illegal and the results invalid. Days later, a sentence of the Constitutional Court confirmed the illegality of the referendum (STC 114/2017, 17 October 2017).

4. With the exception of Navarra, Castilla-León and Cantabria, every Region – named 'Autonomías' or 'Autonomous Community' – have their own Public Media Service, with programmes not only in Spanish but also in Basque, Catalan and Galician regions where these languages are spoken.

C. Social and Cultural Values

5. In respect to Media consumption, 40% of the population read print and digital newspapers every day and 40.8% read at least one magazine (CIS, 2016). In the case of TV, it is estimated that each person spends 191 minutes per day watching TV, with sports programmes dominating at 5,980,000 spectators in 2016 for the Champion League match of Manchester City versus Barcelona. Meanwhile, the average for the most popular programme is 3,500,000 spectators (Barlovento 2016).

§2. The Media Landscape

6. Owing to the significant changes that have taken place between 2009 and 2015 among the Spanish media, a two-step description of the Spanish media landscape is provided. First, the most significant actions undertaken by the main media conglomerates during the said period are explained (providing a dynamic description that helps understand the current situation of each of them), followed by a summarized (static) description of the structure and most relevant scope of action of such conglomerates at present.

A. Overview of Media Markets and Main Actors

1. The Most Significant Actions Undertaken by the Main Media Conglomerates

7. The global financial crisis of 2008 had significant impact upon Spanish media corporations for several reasons. On the one hand, all of them had heavily invested in technological innovation considering the emerging digital landscape and particularly considering the analogue switch-off announced for 2010, as a consequence of which they were greatly indebted. On the other hand, the restructuring in terms of organization, human resources, etc. expected as a result of the technological transition had to be moved forward in light of the economic pressure caused by the dramatic drop in advertising investment. Thus, in 2009 'the [media] industry was deep into a spiral of layoffs; editions, publications, broadcasts and production centres were merged; outsourcing was widely used to reduce and cut down on expenses; the number of legal companies dropped; company headquarters were grouped and streamlined, and administrative and property expenses were optimised' (Almirón 2010). These constituted a set of dramatic changes that transformed the Spanish media landscape. The main features of such a transformation were:

- the predominance of the audiovisual industry from the strategic and economic point of view, to the extent that only the conglomerates which had considerable investments in audiovisual businesses were poised to become relevant actors in the Spanish communication landscape;

- the entry of telecommunications operators into the media industry, such as Telefónica with Movistar + (in 2014) and Vodafone (also in 2014);
- the crisis in the public media sector that both involved a crisis of identity and a lack of strategy to adapt to a new competitive environment strongly influenced by technological innovation.

This transformation is reflected in the structure of the most relevant cross-ownership media conglomerates in 2016 in respect of 2009 (Tables 1 and 2).

Table 1 2009 Media Conglomerates' Cross-Ownership

Company	*Main Stockholders*
Gestevisión Telecinco	Mediaset (52%) Vocento (13%)
Grupo Antena 3 TV	Planeta (22.29%) DeAgustini (22.29%) RTL/Bertelsmann (20%)
La Sexta	Gamp/Imagina (Mediapro y grupo Arbol) (51%) Televisa (40%)
Net TV	Vocento (55%) Intereconomía (25%) Walt Disney (20%)
Corporació Catalana de Comunicació (Avui)	Godó (40%), Generalitat de Cataluña (20%)
Radiopolis (México)	Prisa (50%) Telefónica (17%) Vivendi (5%)
Unión Radio	Prisa (69%) Godó (14%)

Source: Nuria Almirón (2010), information from institutional websites. Almirón, N. Grupos privados propietarios de medios de comunicación en España, principales datos estructurales y financieros, Communication & Society, vol. 22, n. 1.

Table 2 2016 Media Conglomerates' Cross-Ownership

	Main Stockholders
Mediaset España	Mediaset (41.2%) Prisa (18.3%) Vocento (13%)
Atresmedia	Planeta (22.29%) DeAgostini (22.29%) RTL/Bertelsmann (20%) Imagina (Mediapro y Globomedia) (10.2%) FMR LLC (3%)
Movistar +	Telefónica (100%)
Vodafone	Vodafone (100%)
Net TV	Vocento (55%) Walt Disney (20%)

Corporació Catalana de Comunicació (Avui)	Godó (40%), Generalitat de Cataluña (20%)
Prisa Radio	Prisa (73.49%) Godó (18.37%) Trastámara (8.14%)

Note: updated by Ana Azurmendi.

8. In 2009 the Spanish market was characterized both by heavy media concentration (five actors comprised over half of the business) and by the fact that large telecom operators that offered pay audiovisual services were not yet making large profits from such services. In 2015, the concentration of media ownership was even higher, while large *telecom* operators played a significant role in the restructuring of the media market. Three steps were taken towards this transformation.

9. The Telefónica group, under the brand name 'Movistar +', made a strong entry into the Spanish media market. In 2014, it purchased 56% of Canal + (pay television channel owned by Grupo Prisa), being already in possession of 22%, and purchased the remaining 22% from Mediaset. The Comisión Nacional del Mercado y la Competencia (National Commission on Financial Markets and Competition or CNMC) approved this operation in 2015, even though it resulted in Telefónica controlling 85% of the pay television services in Spain and over 70% of subscribers (García Santamaría 2016). Some of the conditions required by the CNMC to Telefónica were: to make up to 50% of its premium channels available to competitors (whether blockbusters by major corporations such as Sony, Warner and Fox or live sport broadcasts); to limit to two years the exclusive exploitation of contents purchased by Telefónica in some broadcast windows, while for others such as emissions in video on demand and series of catalogue no exclusive content can be acquired and no broadcasting rights which the actor does not intend to exploit shall be purchased; to not discriminate in its networks the traffic of Internet-based pay television operators such as those provided by groups such as Yomvi, Filmin, Netflix and Wuaki TV. In 2014, Vodafone, the second Spanish telecom operator, purchased ONO (a telecommunications conglomerate that had been advocating for cable television in Spain since the 1990s).

10. Telecinco Gestevisión, with the purchase of Cuatro Televisión from Prisa in 2010, became Mediaset España. As a result, Prisa became a shareholder alongside Mediaset – the majority shareholder – and Vocento. The Polanco family lost control of the Grupo Prisa, its ownership dropping from 68% to 20%.

11. On the other hand, the Antena 3 group became Atresmedia after the purchase of La Sexta Televisión in 2013, therefore joining traditional shareholders Planeta, DeAgostini and RTLBeterlsman, Imagina Media Audiovisual and an investment fund.

12. These last two operations caused media concentration to grow dramatically, to the point of a media duopoly. In fact, Mediaset España and Atresmedia now gather 57% of the audience and 85% of the advertising revenue (Arranz 2016).

13. Alongside the private media conglomerates, there is also RTVE, the Spanish Public Radio and Television Corporation (Corporación Pública de Radio y Televisión Española), the FORTA (Federation of Regional Radio and Television Bodies in Spain) that groups together twelve out of seventeen regional radio and television bodies representing public media power. It was indeed the economic crisis and the drop in advertising revenue which made private media conglomerates pressurize the government for RTVE to remove all advertising. In 2009, Act 8/2009 on the Financing of the Corporación de Radio y Televisión Española was passed, banning all kinds of advertising (with some specific sponsorship exceptions) in national TV broadcasts. In exchange, telecom operators are required to give 0.9% of their gross annual revenue to the RTVE public corporation, while private television stations must contribute 3% of their annual gross operating income. The stiff competition in the audiovisual industry alongside audience fragmentation owing to the emergence of DTT (Digital Terrestrial Television) and the need for significant investment in technological renovation have had an impact on these media, with a twofold effect: on the one hand, it has brought about a loss of identity caused by the difficulties in offering high-quality – public – contents that the audience may find appealing; on the other hand, its lack of flexibility to adapt to the current circumstances of the industry has been further proven, both in terms of contents, organization and strategy. This has resulted in increased indebtedness (Azurmendi, Manfredi, López Vidales 2012).

14. As for those media conglomerates that prior to the crisis mainly relied on the print media industry, they have been set aside by the three major actors in the Spanish media market: Atresmedia, Mediaset and Movistar +. That is the case of Unidad Editorial, its main asset being the sports daily '*Marca*' and the newspaper '*El Mundo*'; Vocento, with twelve regional dailies and the national newspaper ABC – further to its purchase from the group Prensa Española; Grupo Godó, with 'La Vanguardia' in Catalonia; Zeta with the magazine '*Interviú*' and the regional newspaper '*El Periódico de Cataluña*', as well as Prensa Ibérica, owned by the Moll family, with thirteen regional papers. In fact, while in 2015 television moved EUR 2,011 million in advertising revenue (of which EUR 1,719 million were accounted for by Mediaset and Atresmedia), the advertising revenue from newspapers amounted to 46.5 million (*elmundo.es* 12 December 2016, data from Libro Blanco de la Prensa Diaria AEDE 2016).

15. In addition to being the second actors in the media market, newspaper groups also faced another crisis: the increasing drop in readers and advertising revenue. As pointed out by García Santamaría, 'digital editions have brought about a drop in income and the greater part of newspaper companies have been incapable of implementing feasible methods that would allow them to obtain profits from their online activity'. Regarding newspaper readers, the leading newspaper is the sports daily '*Marca*', with 2.3 million daily readers. The predominant general information newspapers are *El País* (Prisa), with 1,419,000 daily readers, and *El Mundo* (Unidad Editorial) with 852,000 daily readers. As for regional newspapers, highlight is given to *La Vanguardia* (Catalonia) with 634,000 readers, *El Periódico* (Catalonia) with 489,000 daily readers, *La Voz de Galicia* with 589,000 daily readers and *El Correo* (Basque Country) with 411,000 daily readers.

2. The Structure of the Main Media Conglomerates

16. Regarding the structure and scope of action of the main media conglomerates in Spain at present:[1]

17. Grupo Mediaset España Comunicación

PRESIDENT: Alejandro Echevarría Busquet CEO: Paolo Vasile

Mediaset España Comunicación is notable for its television leadership and its expansion across the audiovisual industry, although it is hardly involved in publishing and radio. The Group was founded in 1989, upon the liberalization of the management of television channels in Spain, under the name Gestevisión and under the sponsorship of Fininvest (owned by the Italian media mogul Silvio Berlusconi). The current Group resulted from the merger of Gestevisión-Telecinco and Cuatro (Grupo Prisa) back in 2010.

The main media and fields in which it operates are:

- Television: Telecinco, Cuatro, FDF, La Siete, Energy, Divinity, Boing, Nueve.
- Production companies: Endemol, CINT, Atlas, Alba Adriática, Telecinco Cinema, Producciones Mandarina, Big Bang Media, La fábrica de la Tele, Sogecuatro.
- Advertising and marketing: Publiespaña, GET, Publimsedia Gestión.
- International media: Investments in TV through CaribeVisión.

18. Grupo Atresmedia (Planeta/De Agostini)

PRESIDENT: José Creuheras Margenat CEO: Silvio González Moreno

Since 2013, the group name is Atresmedia, and its main areas of activity comprise Atresmedia Televisión, Atresmedia Radio, Atresmedia Digital, Atresmedia Publicidad and Atresmedia Cine. Alongside these are all of its other brands, such as Fundación Antena 3, a production company specialized in branded content Ver-T, a technological solution and integrated computerized management company I+3 and its Corporate Responsibility undertakings (Ponle Freno, El Estirón, Hazte Eco).

The group, which originates from the Editorial Planeta publishing house (owned by the Lara family), has considerable presence in publishing through Planeta, Seix Barral, Ariel, Ediciones Deusto or Espasa-Calpe. However, for the past decade, it made heavy investments in media – alongside Grupo De Agostini – particularly with the purchase of 25.1% of the capital of Antena 3 and the purchase of Onda Cero (radio station) in 2003. At present, Grupo Planeta and Grupo De Agostini own over 41% of the Group (Atresmedia), therefore being the main shareholders. The remaining 20% is owned by RTL, a subsidiary of the German media conglomerate Bertelsmann.

The main media and fields in which it operates are:

- Publishing houses: Editorial Planeta, Editorial Espasa-Calpe, Ediciones Destino, Seix Barral, Ed. EMECÉ, Ediciones Martínez Roca, Editis Paris, Ediciones Minotauro, Libros Cúpula, Zenith, Editorial Esencia, Timunmas, Destino Infantil,

1. The descriptions of media conglomerates are conducted as per Vidal, J.M. and Barboni, S., Los medios audiovisuales en España, Nota Técnica (Llorente & Cuenca) 2013, as updated by García Santamaría, J.M. 2016 and Azurmendi, A., 2016.

Planeta Junior, Booket, Editorial Ariel, Editorial Crítica, Paidós Iberica, Plawerg Editores, GeoPlaneta, BackList, Planetalector, Yoyo, Destinolibro and Quinteto.

- Newspapers and magazines: *La Razón, Psychologies, Historia y Vida, Lonely Planet, Redes.*
- Television: Antena 3 Tv, Neox, Nitro, Nova, LaSexta, xplora, LaSexta 3, Gol Tv (subscription channel), Ver-Tv (owned by Uniprex Tv, an affiliate company of Antena 3 TV), Marca Tv (50% is owned by La Sexta).
- Radio: Onda Cero, Europa FM, Onda Melodía.
- Magazines: *Psychologies, Historia y Vida, Lonely Planet.*
- Cinema and audiovisual productions: DeAPlaneta, Planeta Junior.
- Book selling: casadellibro.com, Círculo de lectores, Planeta Directo, Shopo.
- International media: in the international landscape, in addition to the editions in Spanish-speaking countries, Portugal, Brazil or France, it also owns Casa Editorial El Tiempo, one of the main media groups in Colombia, owner of the magazine El Tiempo or City TV (Bogotá).

19. Grupo VEO Televisión SA (Unidad Editorial)

PRESIDENT: Antonio Fernández Galiano VICE-PRESIDENT: Gianpaolo Zambeletti

Unidad Editorial resulted from the merger of Grupo Recoletos and Unedisa in 2007. From that point onwards, the new conglomerate was named Unidad Editorial and was 96.31% owned by the Italian conglomerate RCS MediaGroup (owner of Unedisa). This group manages two of the most important newspapers in the Spanish press: El Mundo and Marca (the sports newspaper with the widest outreach in Spain), as well as Expansión, the leading economic newspaper, and Estadio Deportivo, a sports newspaper serving Andalusia. It also has a strong presence in magazines and weekly newspapers. In this regard, we could also mention supplements.

In addition, the group Unidad Editorial offers, through Orbyt, a digital newsstand where publishers can sell their products.

In the television industry, it also operates a multiplex managed by Veo Televisión S.A., one of the awardees of Spanish DTT contracts, owned by Unidad Editorial. Since 2013, it operates the channels Discovery Max and Marca TV, alongside other operators, and it rents two of its frequencies to AXN (Sony) and 13 TV (COPE). The main media and fields in which it operates are:

- Press: Marca, El Mundo, Expansión.
- Television: Marca TV, 13 TV (rented by COPE), MundoInteractivo, Discovery max (rented to DISCOVERY Communications Spain & Portugal, S.L.U.), AXN (rented to Sony Pictures Television Networks Iberia, S.L. subscription channel).
- Magazines: *Telva, Yo Dona, MarcaMotor, Revista oficial de la NBA, ARTE, Diario Médico, Correo Farmacéutico, Actualidad Económica, Aventura de la Historia, Fuera de Serie* (Expansión), *MarcaPlayer* (videogames), *Siete Leguas* (travelling), *Golf Digest, La Luna de Metropoli,* Magazine and *El Cultural.*
- Radio: Radio Marca, esRadio.

20. Sociedad Gestora de Televisión NET TV (Grupo Vocento)

PRESIDENT: Diego de Alcazar Silvela CEO: Luis Enriquez

The Vocento Group was founded in September 2001 after the merger of Grupo Correo (1875), a regional press leader in Spain with twelve regional newspapers, and Prensa Española (1891) owned by the Luca de Tena family, who also owns the national newspaper ABC. This group has multiple media interests in all information and entertainment areas.

Vocento's shares are held by several major shareholders, none of them holding a dominant position. The main shareholder is the Ybarra family, holding 11.07% of the shares through the company Mezouna, S.A., ahead of the Valjarafe S.L. that holds 10.09% and Lima S.L. holding 9.78%.

The main media and fields in which it operates are:

- National and regional newspapers: ABC, Qué!, El Correo, El Diario Vasco, El Diario Montañés, La Verdad, Ideal, Hoy, Sur, La Rioja, El Norte de Castilla, El Comercio, La Voz de Cádiz, Las Provincias. Supplements: XL Semanal, Mujer Hoy, Hoy Corazón.
- Magazines: *Inversión & Finanzas*.
- Television (Net TV): Paramount Channel, Intereconomía TV, MTV, Disney Channel, (La 10 and Metropolitan in regional emissions).
- Radio: ABC Punto Radio.
- Audiovisual Productions: Grupo Europroducciones, BocaBoca Producciones, Videomedia, Tripictures, Hill Valley.

21. Grupo Prisa

PRESIDENT: Juan Luis Cebrián Echarri VICE-PRESIDENT: Fernando Abril-Martorell

Promotora de Informaciones S.A (PRISA) was founded in 1972 by Jesús de Polanco and Francisco Pérez González, although by 2014 the Polanco family only held 20% of shares through the company Rucandio S.A., while Banco Santander, CaixaBank and HSBC held 15% and Amber investors (a US-based vulture fund) held 15.5%.

Grupo Prisa is a leading company in daily press communications through Prisa Noticias, a written press affiliate company of PRISA that owns the general information newspaper El País. On the other hand, in the field of radio broadcasting, it operates the largest radio broadcasting groups in Spain through Prisa Radio.

The main media and fields in which it operates are:

- Press: El País, As, Cinco Días, Rolling Stone, Cinemanía, Revista 40, Claves, Gentleman, Lux, Revista de Vinhos.
- Radio: Cadena SER, Los 40 Principales, M80 Radio, Cadena Dial, Máxima FM, Radio Olé, OnaFM.
- Cinema: Prisa Cine (formerly Sogecine-Sogepaq).
- Publishing houses: Grupo Santillana, comprising: Santillana Educación, Santillana Formación, Richmond Publishing, Alfaguara, Alfaguara Infantil y Juvenil, Taurus, Aguilar, El País-Aguilar, Altea, Punto de Lectura and SUMA.
- Advertising: Gestión de Medios.

- Cultural events and concerts: Planet Events (concert planning), Nova and Lyris & Music (music publishing), GVM Colecciones (DVD and CD commercialization), RLM Rosa Lagarrigue Management (artist representation and agency) and MOS Merchandising On Stage or La Oficina del Autor (management of rights of artists and leisure and entertainment brands).
- International: direct presence in America in the field of radio broadcasting and television in Argentina, Colombia, Costa Rica, Chile, USA, Mexico and Panama. Through the Grupo Media Capital in Portugal, presence in free-access television, NBP production company and the radio of Grupo Media Capital Radio. In France, it holds shares in Le Monde (15%) and Presse Europe Regions (11%) through several regional newspapers.

B. Broadcasting Infrastructure

22. The analogue switch-off took place in April 2010. By such date, the DTT had been around in Spain for twelve years. Despite the expectations around a larger range of channels that would foster pluralism, better market segmentation for advertising targets and a wider democratization of access to premium contents (Casero & García Santamaría), what happened instead was a rather unappealing offer of contents, where shows were repeatedly rebroadcast, the appearance of new channels with poor contents and a dramatic proliferation of local free-access channels – around 1,200. While in 1998 two nationwide and eight regional television channels existed, with the appearance of DTT the number of nationwide private channels came to twenty-four, owned by six media conglomerates, alongside eight public channels by TVE (the Spanish public television). Thus, DTT remodelled the TV landscape in Spain.

23. Cable television growth had been restrained until 1995, when it was legally regulated by virtue of Act 42/1995 on Cable Telecommunications. By such date, the main private television conglomerates – Antena 3, Telecinco, Prisa – had already been involved in the Hertzian television business for several years. Grupo ONO, the heir of Cablevisión led by Eugenio Galdón, was the main group within the industry that showed an interest in audiovisual contents. It was purchased by Vodafone in 2014. Vodafone and Movistar + by Telefónica are the main cable television providers in Spain at present.

24. Satellite TV platform Digital + (resulted from the 2003 merger of the two existing platforms at the time, Vía Digital and Sogecable), purchased by Telefónica in 2014 and has brought satellite broadcasting through Movistar +. However, Telefónica is more interested in cable television, and therefore many of its contents are not offered through satellite.

25. As for turnover, premium television – both satellite and cable – had profits of 622 million, while free-to-access television had a revenue of EUR 441 million and radio services made 77 million during the first quarter of 2016 (Comisión Nacional de los Mercados y la Competencia 2016). When broken down by technology, during the same period the DTT accounted for a total revenue of EUR 442 million, while satellite television profits came up to 337.1 million (Comisión de la Competencia 2016).

26. As for radio, four stations (RNE -public-, SER, COPE and Onda Cero) gathered 90% of the audience. SER concentrated 40% of the total audience and around one-third of advertising (García Santamaría, J.V.). In 2016, radio had 11,211,000 listeners in non-specialty broadcasting and 14,615 for specialty formats (EGM summary February-November 2016 at www.aimc.es/-Datos-EGM-Resumen-General-.html last accessed on 2 January 2016). As pointed out by García Santamaría, in a similar fashion to television, 'the fact that three concurrent companies gather such an audience share leaves hardly any room for other conglomerates and stations to survive'. In addition to this, it is worth noting the hold-up in the development of digital radio resulting from the fact that the technical regulation on radio, enacted by Royal Decree 1287/1999, did not require a total analogue switch-off but instead opted for the coexistence of both digital and analogue technology.

C. Technological and Economic Developments of the Media Markets

27. The evolution of the media market is determined by the need to adapt to young audiences, offering a wider range of options to access contents and a stronger inclination towards participatory media. Multiscreen distribution with contents available for computers, tablets and smartphones also brings about new possibilities involving new formats yet to be explored but with great potential for television. Large television events publicized as shared experiences where audiences can watch the event live and join in through social media are a good example, alongside other uses, very efficient from the audience perspective, such as video on demand. On the other hand, the capacity to customize products based on the processing of personal data brings about interesting opportunities for advertising and marketing and ultimately for media. All media conglomerates are taking steps towards these market trends. Both public media, particularly RTVE through rtve.medialab, as well as commercial media such as Atresmedia, Mediaset and Movistar + are investing resources in multi-platform services for these purposes of 1978, which laid the groundwork for the new democratic system in Spain.

§3. Sources of Media Law

28. Spanish media law has a wide range of legal sources with one main feature: these laws were passed after adoption of the Constitution.

A. Constitution of 1978

29. Article 20:

1. The following rights are recognised and protected:

a) the right to freely express and spread thoughts, ideas and opinions through words, in writing or by any other means of reproduction.
b) the right to literary, artistic, scientific and technical production and creation.
c) the right to academic freedom.
d) the right to freely communicate or receive truthful information by any means of dissemination whatsoever. The law shall regulate the right to the clause of conscience and professional secrecy in the exercise of these freedoms.

2. The exercise of these rights may not be restricted by any form of prior censorship.
3. The law shall regulate the organisation and parliamentary control of the mass communication media under the control of the State or any public agency and shall guarantee access to such media by the significant social and political groups, respecting the pluralism of society and of the various languages of Spain.
4. These freedoms are limited by respect for the rights recognised in this Part, by the legal provisions implementing it, and especially by the right to honour, to privacy, to one's own image and to the protection of youth and childhood.
5. The seizure of publications, recordings and other means of information may only be carried out by means of a court order.

30. Article 18:

A. The right to honour, to personal and family privacy and to one's own image is guaranteed.
B. The home is inviolable. No entry or search may be made without the consent of the householder or a legal warrant, except in cases of *flagrante delicto.*
C. Secrecy of communications is guaranteed, particularly regarding postal, telegraphic and telephonic communications, except in the event of a court order.
D. The law shall restrict the use of data processing in order to guarantee the honour and personal and family privacy of citizens and the full exercise of their rights.

B. Intellectual Property

31. It is important to bear in mind the difference between the European legal concept of intellectual property and the American/British concept. In Europe, intellectual property includes only authors' rights to their works: moral rights (the right to authorship, attribution, anonymity, the use of a different name for authorship and integrity; the right to modify the work, withdraw it from the public sphere and access it even if it becomes private property) and economic rights (copy, delivery, public communication, transformation, e.g., translation, adaptation, versioning). On the other hand, the American/British concept of intellectual property is broader and includes patents, trademarks and copyrights.

32. The main laws on intellectual property are:

(1) Royal Legislative Decree 1/1996, 12 April, the Consolidated Text of the Law on Intellectual Property (*Decreto Legislativo 1/1996, que aprueba el Texto unificado de la Ley de Propiedad Intelectual*).
(2) Criminal Code (*Código Penal*), Article 270.

1. Law on Intellectual Property 1/1996, Amended in 2006 and 2014

33. As has occurred in many other countries, digital piracy has drawn the attention of Spanish lawmakers. In fact, the Law on Intellectual Property (*Ley de Propiedad Intelectual),* the Consolidated Text of the Law on Intellectual Property, adopted by Legislative Decree 1/1996 (*Decreto Legislativo 1/1996, que aprueba el Texto unificado de la Ley de Propiedad Intelectual*), which was first amended in 2006, proved to be ineffective against the massive illegal delivery, downloading and uploading of music and movies on the Internet. The last reform of the Intellectual Property Law, by means of Law 21/2014, attempted to increase effectiveness by using a threefold strategy: (1) Establishing criteria in confusing cases, such as Internet content aggregators and certain copyright limitations; (2) Increasing penalties; (3) Reformulating the competencies of the Intellectual Property Commission (*Comisión de Propiedad Intelectual*), a department of the Ministry of Education, Culture and Sport.

2. Criminal Code, Article 270

34. Article 270 of the Criminal Code (*Código Penal*) also provides for legal protection of intellectual property.

35. It attempts to regulate the main aspects involving intellectual property while taking into account the activities that cause the most harm, such as illegal copying, plagiarism, illegal public communication and delivery, as well as any transformation of an original work and the facilitation of instruments whose specific intention is the unauthorized removal of the means used to protect works protected by copyright.

36. As a result of the 2015 reform involving the amendment of Articles 270 and 271 of the Criminal Code, any act of exploitation without the author's approval could be considered a criminal offence. Any Internet link to the location of illegal works was considered illegal. Article 270 of the Criminal Code increased penalties for criminal infringement of copyright to a cumulative fine or confinement of twelve to twenty-four months in addition to a fine of six to twenty-four months. Article 271 includes aggravated cases.

C. The Media

1. The Press

37. There are no relevant legal provisions specifically on the press. The main regulations applicable to the press are those applicable to other media. Therefore, regardless of the medium through which an attack is made against these rights, the same civil, criminal and constitutional protection is provided for reputation, privacy and one's own image, as well freedom of expression and the right to information.

38. But if the press is understood to be the activity of journalism alone, two important constitutional rights are connected to the independence of journalists: the confidentiality of sources and the clause of conscience (cf. No. 8. Rights of Journalists: Confidentiality of Sources and Clause of Conscience); both of these rights are recognized in Article 20.1.d of the Constitution:

> the right to freely communicate or receive truthful information by any means of dissemination whatsoever. The law shall regulate the right to the clause of conscience and professional secrecy in the exercise of these freedoms.

39. Though the law does not grant individual rights, the Constitutional Court's interpretation of Article 20 of the Constitution assigns a special role to all journalists in fulfilment of the right to information:

> The right to information reaches maximum fulfilment when news professionals are the ones who realize this freedom through the press, the institutional vehicle for forming public opinion, understood in its broadest concept (cf. Constitutional Court Decision STC 165/1987, Legal Argument 10; Constitutional Court Decision STC 168/1986, Legal Argument 2; Constitutional Court Decision STC 199/199, Legal Argument 3; among others).

2. *Television*

40. An incredible number of new laws have been passed in Spain in the last ten years. Some of them were drawn up under pressure from the European Commission, such as the Law on the Reformation of Public Broadcasting Services in 2006 and the Law on Financing Public Broadcasting Services in 2009. Others were adopted for the digital switchover, such as the royal decrees that implemented Law 10/2005 on Urgent Measures to Promote Digital Broadcasting[2] (*Real Decreto 944/2005 de Plan Técnico nacional de la Televisión Digital Terrestre, Real Decreto 945/2005 del Reglamento general de prestación del servicio de televisión digital terrestre*, among others), whose main function was establishing time periods and tasks for TV operators and regional governments. Nevertheless, the most important broadcasting law adopted was General Law 7/2010 on Audiovisual Communication (*Ley 7/2010, General de la Comunicación Audiovisual*), which involved five years of negotiations between the government and the leading Spanish broadcasters (Sogecable, Gestevisión-Telecinco, Antena 3).

2. This law was annulled by Law 7/2010 on Audiovisual Communication, along with many other legal provisions.

a. General Law on Public and Commercial Broadcasting: Law 7/2010 on Audiovisual Communication

41. With the adoption of Law 7/2010 on Audiovisual Communication (*Ley General de la Comunicación Audiovisual*), the regulatory framework of the audiovisual industry was organized after almost thirty years of chaotic and disjointed laws, decrees and other regulations on broadcasting. This was probably the most important thing that Law 7/2010 brought to the Spanish media system: an overriding structure for the broadcasting system.

42. The Law on Audiovisual Communication regulates public and commercial TV and radio broadcasting. It originally provided for the creation of CEMA, the National Council for Audiovisual Media (*Consejo Estatal de Medios Audiovisuales*), but provisions for the council were ultimately removed from the final law. The law also increased the protection of children and the fight against fraudulent advertising. Measures to promote pluralism were included in Article 36. In a concession to commercial TV operators, the law offered the possibility of selling a broadcasting licence to another TV operator. Finally, the law also included a list of infringements and penalties that the CEMA was in charge of applying.

The structure of Law 7/2010 on Audiovisual Communication is as follows:

TITLE I General provisions

TITLE II Basic regulation for audiovisual communication

CHAPTER I Audience's rights

CHAPTER II TV-radio operators' rights

TITLE III Basic regulation for audiovisual market coordination

CHAPTER I Basic regulation for the provision of audiovisual communication services in a plural, transparent market

CHAPTER II Freedom to receive foreign audiovisual communication services

TITLE IV The Public Audiovisual Communication Service

TITLE V The National Council for Audiovisual Media (CEMA) (repealed)

TITLE VI Penalty System

43. Although the main content of Law 7/2010 was the result of the implementation of European Directive 2007/65/EC on Audiovisual Media Services, the Law on Audiovisual Communication went beyond the European legislation in that it truly reorganized the audiovisual media industry.

b. Public Broadcasting Services

44. In the European process of redefining public broadcasting services, the Spanish Public Radio/TV Corporation (RTVE) was reformed by Law 17/2006 on the Reform of Public Radio and Television Services (*Ley de Reforma de la Radio y la Televisión de Titularidad pública*). It was the first time that commercial radio and TV were not included on the list of 'essential public services' (*servicio público esencial*), and were consequently no longer subject to the remit of public audiovisual services. Since the adoption of Law 17/2006, only public radio/TVs are subject to this legal concept:

45. Article 2.1. 'The State's public radio and television service is an essential service for the community and the cohesion of the democratic system; its object is the production, edition and diffusion of a set of radio and television channels with diverse and balanced programmes for all kinds of audiences covering all types of contents, and designed to satisfy Spanish society's need for information, culture, education and entertainment; to promote Spanish cultural identity and diversity; to stimulate the "information society"; and to promote pluralism, participation and other constitutional values while guaranteeing social and significant political groups access to public radio and television.'

46. Article 2.2. 'The function of public service embraces the production of content and the edition and diffusion of open or codified thematic and general channels in the national and international area, as well as the provision of connected or interactive services orientated towards achieving the aims mentioned in the previous paragraph.'

47. The public remit of these radio/TVs is described in Article 3.2.:

a) To promote knowledge and the spreading of constitutional principles and civic values.
b) To guarantee objective, accurate and plural information; it must comply with the criteria of professional independence and political, social and ideological pluralism existing in our society; and it must clearly distinguish between fact and opinion.
c) To facilitate democratic discussion and freedom of expression.
d) To promote democratic participation by guaranteeing the right to access.
e) To promote territorial cohesion and the linguistic and cultural plurality and diversity of Spain.
f) To promote the diffusion and knowledge of Spanish cultural productions, particularly audiovisual productions.
g) To monitor the conservation of historic audiovisual files.

h) To address the widest audience and ensure maximum continuity and geographic and social coverage with a commitment to offering quality, diversity and innovation while complying with ethical requirements.
i) To promote the values of peace.
j) To promote knowledge, safeguard and respect ecological values, and protect the environment.
k) To preserve children's rights.

48. Law 8/2009 on Financing RTVE (*Ley 8/2009 de Financiación de la Corporación de Radio y Televisión Española)* went one step beyond the Law on the Reform of Public Radio and Television Services. Its main new feature was the prohibition of using advertising to finance RTVE. Nevertheless, this measure had a counterpart in the same legal provision. Articles 5.4, 6.4 and 6.5 stipulated compulsory payments to RTVE by telecommunication operators (0.9% of their gross revenue for one year) and commercial TV operators (3% of their gross revenue for one year). The telecoms contested the measure with the European institutions. Finally, on 10 November 2016, the European Court of Justice confirmed that this method of financing the Spanish public television system (RTVE) 'is compatible with the EU rules regarding State aid' (ECLI:EU:C:2016:848, Case C-449/14 P).

c. Public Regional Broadcasting

49. Spain has one of the widest regional audiovisual systems in Europe. Not even Germany with 10 'Länder' television channels can compare to the volume of contents and the organization of regional television channels in Spain. At present, there are 12 public corporations – upon the closing of Canal 9 in Valencia in 2014 – governed by their own regional regulations.[3] Bearing in mind that the combination of the financial crisis, audiovisual market atomization as a result of DTT and the impact of the Internet created a situation fraught with difficulty for national public television, these factors were an actual tsunami for regional television.

50. In spite of the negative atmosphere of opinion surrounding regional television, the contributions of these channels to the local audiovisual industrial fabric, in areas such as production, distribution and promotion of creative talent; have been and still are irreplaceable. Particularly in the cases[4] of EITB, CCMA-TV3, and CRTVG in their capacity as the main promoters of Basque, Catalan and Galician correspondingly. Regional television fulfils its public mission to build citizenship, community and identity by means of local journalism, which develops these tasks not only effectively but also with considerable credibility. Yet, in many cases, economic imbalances and the lack of independence from political parties have been the subject of criticism against regional television. Therefore, it has been required – and still is required – medium-term efforts so their public mission is fulfilled efficiently and under good

3. In Galicia, Asturias, Basque Country, Aragón, Catalonia, Madrid, Castilla-La Mancha, Extremadura, Andalusia, Murcia, the Balearic Islands and the Canary Islands.
4. EITB, Euskal Irrati Telebista, public television in the Basque Country; CCMA-TV3, Corporacio Catalana de Mitjans Audiovisuals, TV3, public television in Catalonia; and CRTVG, Corporación de Radio e Televisión de Galicia, public television in Galicia.

governance. These being the concerns addressed by European Union (EU) measures on public audiovisual services since 1998.

51. The passing of Act 6/2012 to 'amend the General Act on Audiovisual Media to make management methods of regional audiovisual media services more flexible' has brought about considerable opportunities to outsource regional public television services and to privatize their management. The concern about this act also regards the possible effect of these regional televisions disappearing.

52. However, two different groups can be found among these corporations: those who offer contents in languages other than Spanish and therefore play a very important role for culture and identity, and those who do not have this differentiating factor.

d. Regional Public Regional Radio/TVs with Programmes in Languages Other Than Spanish: EITB (Basque Country), CCMC (Catalonia), RTVG (Galicia), IB3 (Balearic Islands)

53. In the case of the Spanish regions (*Comunidades Autónomas*) with their own language, the laws on regional public radio/TV are focused on this important sign of identity.[5] One of the main purposes of public broadcasting services is to consolidate the use of regional languages: Basque (spoken in the Basque Country and Navarre) and Catalan (spoken in Catalonia and the Balearic Islands) and Galician (spoken in Galicia). However, there are some differences in the roles attributed to the language and the public media outlet. For example, the laws of the Basque Country, Catalonia and Galicia consider the regional language and its use by public media to be an essential expression of the region's political, cultural and social identity. This is not the case in the law of the Balearic Islands, where Catalan is understood as a means of cultural merging with Catalonia rather than an element of regional identity.

54. The most important laws on regional public radio/TV in regions where a language is spoken other than Spanish are:

- *Basque Country*
  Ley 5/1982, de creación del Ente Público Radio Televisión Vasca
- *Catalonia*
  Ley 11/2007, de la Corporación Catalana de Medios Audiovisuales
  Ley 22/2005, de la Comunicación Audiovisual de Cataluña
- *Galicia*
  Ley 9/2011, de los Medios Públicos de Comunicación Audiovisual de Galicia
- *Balearic Islands*
  Ley 15/2010, del Ente Público de Radiotelevisión de las Illes Balears.

5. Canal 9, the public TV outlet in Valencia, was closed in November 2014. There is currently a project under way to launch it again, but it has not yet been implemented.

e. Regional Public Radio/TVs with Programming only in Spanish: Canal Sur (Andalusia), Aragón Televisión (Aragon), PATV (Asturias), RTVC (Canary Islands), CMTV (Castilla-La Mancha), CETV (Extremadura), Telemadrid (Madrid) and RTRM (Murcia)

55. An examination of the regional laws on regional public broadcasting in regions where Spanish is the only language spoken makes it difficult to justify a regional public broadcasting service when the nationwide broadcasting service is operating at the same time.[6] What are the differences between them? What is the specific mission of regional public radio/TV? However, even if the regional differences are real, they may not be strong enough to create a unique identity in and by themselves.

56. All of these regional laws include references to the region's own cultural traditions and yet they seem insufficient to justify the need to create and maintain a regional radio/TV, especially in an unsustainable economy. The legal provisions below have this feature in common: the regions lack sufficient signs of identity to support the creation and maintenance of a regional public radio/TV station. This lack of identity even makes it difficult to justify the concept of 'public mission' for these types of radio/TVs.

57. Regional regulations on public broadcasting services in regions without an official regional language include the following laws:

- Andalusia. Ley de la Comunidad Autónoma de Andalucía 18/2007, de la Radio y Televisión de titularidad autonómica gestionada por la Agencia Pública Empresarial de la Radio y Televisión de Andalucía (RTVA).
- Aragon. Ley 8/1987, de Creación, organización y control parlamentario de la Corporación Aragonesa de Radio y Televisión.
- Asturias. Ley del Principado de Asturias 2/2003, de Medios de Comunicación Social.
- Canary Islands. Ley 13/2014, de Radio y Televisión Públicas de la Comunidad Autónoma de Canarias.
- Castilla-La Mancha. Ley 3/2000, de Creación del Ente Público de Radio-Televisión de Castilla-La Mancha.
- Extremadura. Ley 3/2008, de 16 de junio, reguladora de la Empresa Pública Corporación Extremeña de Medios Audiovisuales.
- Madrid. Ley 8/2015, de 28 de diciembre, de Radio Televisión Madrid.
- Murcia. Ley de la C.A. de Murcia 9/2004, de 29 de diciembre, sobre Creación de la Empresa Pública Regional Radio Televisión de la Región de Murcia.

f. Cable TV

58. Many plans for the cable industry were delayed and eventually discontinued when the government made the decision in 1995 to promote aerial broadcasting (analogue and digital, terrestrial and satellite) instead of cable. At that time, Telefónica

6. Although Aragonese is spoken in Aragon and Asturian is spoken in Asturias, these regional languages are not considered 'official languages' and the broadcasting laws in these regions are therefore more similar to those in this group.

– the telecommunications operator that held the monopoly in Spain for decades – was in a privileged situation among competitors on the cable market. There were probably political reasons behind this particular option, but another explanation for the decision was the desire to help RTVE, whose debts had been increasing since 1989, the year that commercial television outlets entered the TV market. The panorama of a weak public television surrounded by thirty or forty commercial TV outlets was simply inconceivable at that time in both political and economic terms. By maintaining the analogue aerial TV market as the only market, competition could be reduced. In fact, *TVE 1* and *TVE 2* (the two public TV outlets) were competing against three commercial TVs: Telecinco, Antena 3 and the pay channel Canal+.

59. This trend changed with the adoption of General Law 32/2003 on Telecommunications (*Ley 32/2003, General de Telecomunicaciones*), which provided for liberalization of all TV and radio cable services starting on 31 December 2009. Finally, Decree 920/2006 on General Regulation for Cable service of TV and Radio (*Reglamento general de prestación del servicio de difusión de radio y televisión por cable*) moved the date for this liberalization forward to 2006.

60. But the most important change in the audiovisual landscape has been the entry of telecommunications operators into the audiovisual market by virtue of the General Telecommunications Act 9/2014, of 9 May. The first measure passed by virtue of this act is the so-called 'Digital Dividend', consisting of the release of the electromagnetic spectrum used by televisions in favour of telecom operators. The rationale provided in the preamble to this act is that televisions were under-using the spectrum available. As per the same conditions established by the Technical Plan of 2005, distribution at present remains as follows:

(1) *Private television:* Four multiplexes, the use of which is assigned to (Article 5.1):

- *Net TV*: half of the national multiplex MPE1
- *Veo TV*: half of the national multiplex MPE1
- *Atresmedia*, in respect of the licence held by *Antena 3*: half of the MPE2 multiplex
- *Atresmedia*, in respect of the licence held by *La Sexta*: half of the MPE2 multiplex
- *Mediaset*, in respect of the licence held by *Gestevisión*: half of the MPE3 multiplex and a quarter of the MPE4 multiplex
- *Mediaset*, in respect of the licence held by *Cuatro*: half of the MPE3 multiplex and a quarter of the MPE4 multiplex
- *RTVE*, the Corporación de Radio y Televisión Española, will be assigned the capacity of national coverage multiplex RGE1 and two thirds of the capacity of the national coverage multiplex RGE2 for the purpose of rendering the public service of television audiovisual media (section 4. 1)

(2) *Regional television:* Assigned a regional coverage multiplex – MAUT. The Act contemplates the possibility of using the multiplex of private companies managing television services within said area on a licensed basis.

61. As a result, broadcasting space is now free for telecommunications companies and its audiovisual content distribution sub lessees to conduct their business. It has not been even a year since the General Telecommunications Act was passed and the war between content platforms has already started, leaving traditional television channels empty-handed. *Movistar* and *Netflix* are currently struggling to gather the greatest amount of users. The former with exclusive rights over the football league, the Champions League (between January 2016 and January 2019) and 10,000 titles through Yomvi, while the latter is (theoretically) offering 14,000 films and series. *Orange* and *Vodafone* follow the steps of *Movistar*. Television including TV on demand, exclusive contents, sports, music and social networks is an emerging reality yet to develop its full potential.

g. Digital Television

62. Between 1998 and 2005, a considerable number of decrees on technical aspects and deadlines were adopted until Law 10/2005 on Urgent Measures towards the Promotion of DTT, the Liberalization of Cable TV and the Promotion of Pluralism (*Ley de Medidas Urgentes para el Impulso de la Televisión Digital Terrestre, de Liberalización de la Televisión por Cable y de Fomento del Pluralismo*) was passed, with its complementary Decree 945/2005 on adoption of the General Regulation of the DTT Service. Paradoxically, one of the first initiatives of the 2005 law was the reform of the 1988 Law on Commercial TV, with the addition of two more analogue radio/TVs, ultimately awarded to La Cuatro (Sogecable) and La Sexta (Mediapro). These corporations were later taken over by the predominant TV companies Telecinco and Antena 3. After the merger, their name was changed to Mediaset (which took over La Cuatro four years after it was launched) and Atresmedia (which took over La Sexta six years after its premiere). This merger went against the aim of the Law on Urgent Measures, i.e., to increase the number of players on the TV market by the time the digital switchover took place on 3 April 2010.

63. Decree 944/2005 distributed multiplexes as per below:

I. Private television: all existing private television channels would have a programme at one nationwide multiplex, with no possibility of regional variation; the same licensing obligations would apply, i.e. broadcasting would be free-access or encrypted depending on each case.

II. RTVE: a nationwide multiplex would be reserved for direct operation, with the possibility of offering regional variations, as well as a national digital programme without regional variation options.

III. Regional television:

   a. Each of the Autonomous Communities would have a regional multiplex and the capacity to conduct regional variations at a province level. If technical conditions – involving the availability of the radio spectrum – allowed another multiplex, they would be in the position to manage such.

b. Autonomous Communities would be able to decide which programmes belonged to public regional television and which programmes offered by private companies were broadcast under concessions. However, the whole multiplex being fully managed by the public administration would also be a possibility. In such a case, authorisation by the Central Government would be required.

c. The requirement to obtain a new concession for existing regional television stations under private management was established.

64. The General Regulation on the Provision of DTT Services enacted by means of Royal Decree 945/2005 established the *título habilitante* (broadcasting licence) as a basic legal requirement to exploit digital television, to be either issued by the Government – if national coverage – or by Autonomous Communities for regional or local coverage (Article 3 of the Regulation).

3. Radio

a. From Isolation to a Coordination Plan With the IUT

65. Until 1978, there simply was no legal framework for the Spanish radio system. Because Spain was not a member of the International Union of Telecommunications (IUT), the standard situation in every Spanish regional dial was a chaotic state of radio interference. Another decisive factor that determined future regulation of radio was the fact that, from the very beginning, the first radios in the country were private businesses operating without a licence. In 1978, order was imposed thanks to two consecutive Technical Plans (*Planes Técnicos*) adopted by decrees in 1978 and 1979. Another definitive step in the harmonization of the radio dial took place when the Spanish regions, and even some cities, began participating in the design of the national radio map, thanks to Law 31/1987 on Organisation of Telecommunications (*Ley de Organización de las Telecomunicaciones)* and Law 11/1991 on Organisation and Control of Local Radio Stations (*Ley de Organización y Control de las Emisoras Municipales de Radiodifusión Sonora*).

b. Public Radio as a Public Service

66. Another important turning point in the new national radio map in Spain was the discontinuation of the concept of 'essential public service' (*servicio público esencial*) originally applied to all public and commercial radio stations as a result of Law 17/2006 on the Reform of Public Radio and Television Services (*Ley de Reforma de la Radio y la Televisión de titularidad pública*). As had occurred with public TV, advertising was prohibited on public radio stations by Law 8/2009 on Financing RTVE (*Ley de Financiación de la Radio y la Televisión Española).*

67. Law 7/2010 on Audiovisual Communication completed this panorama in the sense that the law discontinued application of the concept of 'public service' to all outlets by introducing the concept of 'service of general interest'.

c. Digital Radio

68. Implementation of digital radio in Spain was different from implementation of digital TV. Implementation of digital radio did not include the complete discontinuation of the analogue system. Decree 1287/1999 on Technical Plan for Nationwide Digital Terrestrial Radio (*Plan Técnico nacional de la Radiodifusión Sonora Digital Terrenal*) set the date for digital radio switchover for 2006, but for only 85% of the population. In the reformed Decree of 2011, anticipated coverage was only 20%.

4. Internet

a. Regulation Principles

69. In accordance with the European Directive on Information Society Services and Electronic Commerce 2000/31/EC, the Internet is regulated in Spain by Law 34/2002 on the Information Society and Electronic Commerce (*Ley de la Sociedad de la Información y del Comercio Electrónico).* This law is inspired by two principles: (1) The process of 'notice and take down', which prioritizes collaboration among telecommunication operators and authorities so that rules can be effectively applied to the Internet; and (2) Laws existing in the real world may be applied to the virtual world, thus promoting the principle of complementarity between Law 34/2002 on the Information Society and Electronic Commerce and all other legal regulations on the media:

> Article 1.2. 'The provisions of this law shall be understood without prejudice to the provisions of any national or autonomous community regulations outside the coordinated regulatory environment or whose purpose is the protection of public health and safety, including safeguarding the national defence, consumers' interests, the tax system applicable to information society services, the protection of personal data and regulations on the defence of fair competition'.

> Article 13.1. 'The providers of information society services are subject to civil, criminal and administrative liability, as generally established in the legal system, without prejudice to the provisions of this law'.

b. Cybercrime

70. In 2010, Spain ratified the European Convention on Cybercrime,[7] in force since 2004, aiming to prosecute more effectively those crimes committed through the Internet, such being:

(a) White hat hacking: accessing network systems or corporate, institutional or personal computers without causing any damage.

7. Available at http://conventions.coe.int/Treaty/Commun/QueVoulezVous.asp?NT=185&CL=ENG.

(b) Destructive hacking: computer sabotage.
(c) Interception of information systems.
(d) Internet scams.
(e) The creation and spreading of virus.
(f) The spreading or distribution of child pornography.
(g) Copyright infringement.

71. Simultaneously, enacted even prior to the ratification of this Treaty, the Spanish Criminal Code contains a series of criminal actions conducted on the Internet, such as:

(a) computer sabotage, including the spreading of viruses through the Internet:[8] 'Article 264.1. Whoever, by any means, without authorisation and in a serious way, were to erase, damage, deteriorate, alter, suppress or make data, computer programs or electronic documents pertaining to others inaccessible, if the result produced is serious, shall be punished with a prison sentence of six months to three years.'
(b) piracy of services through the Internet:

Article 286: 1. Punishment by imprisonment of six months to two years and a fine from six to twenty-four months shall be handed down to whoever, without the consent of the service provider and for commercial purposes, provides intelligible access to a radio or television broadcasting sound or image service, to interactive services provided remotely by electronic means, or who provides conditional access to these, considered as an independent service, by means of:

• Manufacturing, importation, distribution, making available by electronic means, sale, rental or possession of any computer equipment or programme that is unauthorised in another member State of the European Union, designed or adapted to make such access possible.

• Installation, maintenance or replacement of the equipment or computer programmes mentioned in paragraph 1.

2. An identical punishment shall be applied to whoever, for profit, were to alter or duplicate the identifying number of telecommunications equipment or sell equipment that has undergone fraudulent manipulation.

8. Through the amendment of the Spanish Criminal Code, enacted by virtue of Act 1/2015, new articles have been added, namely 264.2 and 264*bis* setting out aggravating circumstances of crimes, and 264*ter* and 264*quarter* regarding those persons who facilitate the perpetration of the aforesaid crimes, whether a natural or legal person. Article 573.2 sets out the possibility that the aforesaid crimes can be considered as crimes of terrorism.

For the rest of crimes – interception of information, Internet scams, possession and dissemination of child pornography and any other action against intellectual property, the offence types described on a general basis in the Criminal Code shall be adequate.

D. Commercial Speech

72. Commercial speech in Spain is considered separate from the conceptual area of freedom of expression, as concluded by the Constitutional Court in 1989: 'Article 20 (of the Constitution) does not protect the diffusion of commercials as part of a fundamental right because in these kinds of messages the main aim is to point out the existence of a professional activity with a lucrative purpose instead of simply expressing thoughts, ideas and opinions' (17 April 1989, Court Decision, Casado Coca Case).

73. The corpus on commercial speech legislation includes:

I. General Law 34/1988 on Advertising (*Ley General de Publicidad*);
II. Royal Legislative Decree 1/2007, the Consolidated Text of the Law on Consumer and User Defence and Complementary Laws (Real Decreto Legislativo, texto refundido de la Ley General para la defensa de los consumidores y usuarios y otras leyes complementarias)
III. Law 3/1991 (amended in 2009) on Unfair Competition (*Ley de Competencia Desleal*)
IV. Chapter on Advertising in Law 7/2010 on Audiovisual Communication (*Ley General de la Comunicación Audiovisual*)

1. Illegal Advertising

a. Illegal Advertising in Law 34/1988 on Advertising

74. In accordance with the Law on Advertising, the following are illegal acts: (a) any kind of advertisements that ignore human dignity and the values and human rights recognized in the Spanish Constitution, including the protection of children; (b) advertising targeted at children that in any way causes untruthful or risky situations for children; advertising that makes children ask their parents to buy specific goods; and advertising that promotes stereotypical gender situations; (c) unfair advertising; (d) misleading, unfair and subliminal advertising.

75. Article 3. The following is illegal:

• Advertising that infringes a person's dignity or damages the values and rights recognised in the Constitution, especially in Articles 14, 18 and 20.4. The foregoing shall include advertisements that portray women in a discriminatory or degrading manner, either by particularly and directly making use of the female body or parts thereof as a mere object unrelated to the product being promoted, or by associating women's image with stereotypical behaviour that undermines the foundations of our legal system by helping generate the violence referred to in the Law for Comprehensive Protection Measures against Gender-Based Violence.

• Advertising directed at minors that encourages them to purchase a good or service by exploiting their inexperience or credulity, and advertising in which children try to persuade their parents or guardians to make a purchase. Children may not be presented in dangerous situations without a well-founded reason. Advertising shall not be misleading about product features, product safety or the capacities or skills required by children to use the product without causing harm to themselves or third parties.

• Subliminal advertising.

• Advertising that infringes the regulations on advertising certain products, goods, activities or services.

• Misleading advertising, unfair advertising and aggressive adverting, which shall be considered acts of unfair competition, as defined in the Law on Unfair Competition.

b. Illegal Advertising in Law 3/1991 (Amended in 2009) on Unfair Competition

76. Pursuant to the Law on Unfair Competition, the following is illegal: (a) misleading advertising and (b) direct or indirect advertising, information or any activity linked to a company or institution that represents unfair competition.

c. Misleading Advertising

77. Article 5. 'Any conduct containing false information or information that, although true, due to its contents or presentation is or may be misleading for its recipients, such being in the position to change their economic behaviour (...) shall be deemed unfair for its misleading nature'.

78. Article 25. 'Promoting a product or service similar to that commercialised by a company or professional intending to lead consumers or users to believe that such product or service is provided by the said company or professional, this being untrue, shall be deemed unfair for its misleading nature'.

79. Article 26. 'Including communications to promote a product or service as information in the media, such promotion being subject to payment by the company or professional, without expressly setting out in the contents or through images or sounds clearly understandable by consumers or users that such promotion constitutes advertising content shall be deemed unfair for its misleading nature'.

d. Provisions of the Criminal Code on Misleading Advertising

80. Article 282. 'Manufacturers or traders who make false claims or declare untrue features in their offers or publicity of products or services, so as to cause serious, manifest harm to consumers, without prejudice to the relevant punishment for having committed other criminal offences, shall be punished with a sentence of imprisonment of six months to one year or fine from twelve to twenty-four months.'

e. Direct or Indirect Advertising, Information, or Any Activity Linked to a Company or Institution That Represents Unfair Competition

81. Article 9. 'Making or spreading statements on the activity, services, establishment or commercial relationships of a third party that can be detrimental to its reputation in the market shall be deemed unfair, unless they are accurate. Particularly, statements addressing the nationality, beliefs or ideology, private life or any other strictly personal circumstances of the party affected shall not be deemed appropriate.'

82. Article 12. 'Taking unfair advantage, in favour of one self or of a third party, of the advantages of the industrial, commercial or professional reputation acquired by another party in the market shall be deemed as unfair. Precisely, using distinctive marks owned by others or false denominations of origin accompanied by the actual origin of the product or expressions such as *models, system, type, class* and the alike shall be deemed unfair.'

f. Comparative Advertising

83. Comparative advertising is permitted under some conditions established in the Law on Unfair Competition:

84. Article 10:

> Public comparison, including comparative advertising, by means of explicit or implicit reference to a competitor shall be permitted when the following conditions are met:

(a) It compares goods or services intended for the same purpose or meeting the same needs.
(b) It objectively compares one or more material, relevant, verifiable and representative features of those goods and services, which may include price.
(c) For products recognised under a denomination of origin or geographical indication, specific denomination or traditional speciality guaranteed, comparison shall only be permitted with other products with the same designation.
(d) It does not present goods or services as imitations or replicas of goods or services bearing a protected trade mark or trade name.

(e) Comparison shall not contravene the provisions under articles 5, 7, 9, 12 and 20 on acts of deceit, denigration and unfair advantage of the reputation of others.

g. Absolute Prohibition of Advertising of Certain Goods and Services

85. Tobacco, spirits and, in general, alcoholic drinks over 20% ABV may not be advertised in any form on any media. But this prohibition is extended in some cases to places where the sale of cigarettes or alcoholic drinks is prohibited (e.g., schools and universities).

h. Prior Authorization Needed for Some Advertising

86. In some cases, legal provisions call for prior authorization to advertise goods and services related to banks and health. More exhaustive regulations have been published concerning these markets.

E. Reputation

87. Spanish law has a long tradition of criminal protection of the right to reputation. Until 1982, the Criminal Code (*Código Penal*) was the only legal provision that addressed defamation (expressed as the concepts defamation and slander). Law 1/1982 on Civil Protection of the Right to Reputation, Privacy and One's Own Image (*Ley Orgánica 1/1982, de Protección Civil del Derecho al Honor, a la Intimidad personal y familiar y a la propia Imagen*) enacted civil protection of this right.

1. Criminal Protection of Reputation

88. In accordance with Spanish regulations, there are two main acts against the reputation of third parties: to falsely attribute an offence to a third party (orally, in writing or in the press, etc.), which constitutes the crime of defamation; and to insult somebody in an offensive way, which constitutes the crime of slander. This division may seem somewhat vague, but the second form involves falsely attributing acts that are not crimes, but simply bad actions.

89. Article 205. 'Slander involves accusing another person of a felony while knowing it is false or recklessly disregarding the truth.' The addition of 'recklessly disregarding the truth' clearly shows the need for intentionality to lie to commit defamation or at least implicit consent with the fact that defamation occurs.

90. Article 208. 'Defamation is the action or expression that harms the dignity of another person, detracting from his reputation or attacking his self-esteem.'

91. The major difference between slander and defamation in the legal process is that, in the case of slander, criminal liability disappears if the accusation proves to be true.

92. Article 207. 'Whoever is accused of the offence of slander shall be exempt from all punishment by proving the criminal act of which he has accused the other person.'

93. Circumstances that can increase liability in cases of defamation and slander include: the involvement of the media (Article 211) and committing defamation and slander for a price, award or promise (Article 213).

94. In terms of legal punishment, the Criminal Code penalties are severe: (1) If defamation or slander is committed through the media: two years of imprisonment or fines of a duration of six to twenty-four months; (2) if a price, award or promise is involved: special suspension from working as a journalist for six months to two years; (3) if the defamation or slander is acknowledged in front of the judge by the defendant, the possibility of imprisonment or suspension is cancelled (cf. Article 214); (4). the plaintiff's forgiveness cancels any criminal liability (Article 215.3). This is a direct promotion of prejudicial agreement in cases of defamation and slander.

2. Civil Protection of Reputation

95. As mentioned above, Law 1/1982 on Civil Protection of the Right to Reputation, Privacy and One's Own Image is the main source of civil protection for these human rights: Article 7.3: 'The disclosure of facts related to the private life of a person or family that affect the person or family's reputation and good name (…).'

Article 7.7. 'The attribution of facts or the declaration of value judgments through actions or expressions that in any way harm another person's dignity, diminish his/her fame or go against his/her self-esteem.'

96. The same behaviour is covered by both the Criminal Code and civil law, but there are some subtle differences: first, the privacy-reputation link (Article 7.3); second, the classification of offences against reputation into two types, attributions of facts and the statement of opinions, rather than defamation and slander, as in the Criminal Code.

F. Privacy

97. Privacy is a value that is receiving increased protection in Spanish legislation. The first law protecting privacy was Law 1/1982 on Civil Protection of the Right of Reputation, Privacy and One's Own Image (*Ley Orgánica de Protección Civil del Derecho al Honor, a la Intimidad personal y familiar y a la propia Imagen*). The 1995 edition of the Criminal Code (*Código Penal*) then included criminal acts against privacy. As in the case of reputation, the Constitution of 1978 dealt with privacy by establishing basic protection of the human rights that sometimes define the limits of freedom of expression: Article 18.1 'The right to reputation, to personal and family privacy, and to one's own image is guaranteed.'

98. And in Article 20, which defines the limits to freedom of expression and to right to information: Article 20.4. 'These freedoms are limited by respect for the rights recognised in this Part, by the legal provisions implementing it, and especially by the right to reputation, to privacy, to one's own image and to the protection of youth and childhood.'

1. The Protection of Privacy in the Criminal Code

99. The Criminal Code protects privacy on two different levels: (a) general; (b) specified matters related to digital technology.

100. Privacy in general: it provides for punishment for the acts of appropriation of documents, letters, messages, personal documents, and sound and video recordings, and the use of technical elements to get them, when the aim of doing so is to trespass privacy: Article 197.1. 'Whoever, in order to discover the secrets or to breach the privacy of another, without his consent, seizes his papers, letters, electronic mail messages or any other documents or personal belongings, or intercepts his telecommunications or uses technical devices for listening, transmitting, recording or playing sound or image, or any other communication signal, shall be punished with imprisonment of one to four years and a fine of twelve to twenty-four months.'

101. Privacy in specific matters related to digital technology: particularly electronic activity and databases. The Criminal Code (*Código Penal*) describes criminal behaviour that is possible with computers, such as accessing, appropriation, using and modifying the personal data in databases, and transferring, diffusion and disclosure of that data. Article 197.2. 'The same penalties shall be imposed upon whoever, without being authorized, seizes, uses or amends, to the detriment of a third party, reserved data of a personal or family nature of another that are recorded in computer, electronic or telematic files or media, or in any other kind of file or public or private record. The same penalties shall be imposed on whoever, without being authorised, accesses these by any means, and whoever alters or uses them to the detriment of the data subject or a third party.'

2. Privacy in Law 1/1982 on Civil Protection of the Right to Reputation, Privacy and One's Own Image

102. Privacy is a right whose roots are firmly based in human dignity. It has to do with the personal decision about communicating certain personal aspects of one's one life to other persons. Consent in any case is decisive in order to determine the legality or illegality of the acts catalogued by the law as invasion of privacy: Article 7:

> The following shall be considered breach of the protective environment provided for in Article 2 hereof:

(a) The placement of listening and filming devices, as well as optical devices or any other means for recording or reproducing the private life of third parties.
(b) The use of listening devices, optical devices or any other means for learning about the private life of third parties or statements or private letters not addressed to the person making use of such means, as well as taping, recording or reproducing said private life.
(c) The dissemination of facts concerning the private life of a person or family that could affect the person or family's reputation and good name, as well as the

disclosure or publication of the content of letters, memoirs or other personal documents of a private nature.

(d) The disclosure of a person or a family's private data acquired through the professional or official activity of the disclosing party.

(e) Recording, reproducing or publishing by means of photography, film or any other procedure, the likeness of a person in places or at times in and out of his/her private, except in the cases provided for in Article 8.2.

G. Data Protection

1. Data Protection: Data Protection Act 1999 (Ley 15/1999 de Protección de Datos personales')

103. In the same way that the success of Warren and Brandeis' concept of the 'right to privacy' was due to the new risks resulting from photographic technology, especially when applied by the media, the interaction of digital communication in the 1990s brought a new kind of threat to private life, and as a consequence, has generated a new kind of right: the right to personal data protection. The main question at the time was not only privacy – which was sometimes in danger – but the real risk of manipulation in that somebody – the state, police, companies, banks, political parties, different public departments involving health, labour, etc. – could affect individuals, creating exhaustive and specific profiles (with aspects related to a variety of interests in the institutions and businesses above). When looking at this threat, the EU enacted three important directives, all of which are focused on different aspects of personal data protection:

(1) Directive 95/46/EC, (on Personal Data) 'on the Protection of Individuals with regard to the processing of Personal Data and the free movement of such Data'.

(2) Directive 2002/58/EC (on Privacy and Electronic Communications) 'concerning the Processing of Personal Data and the Protection of Privacy in the Electronic Communications'.

(3) Directive 2006/24/EC (on the Retention of Data) 'on the Retention of Data Generated or Processed in connection with the Provision of Publicly available Electronic Communications Services or of Public Communications Networks'.

104. Following these European normative directions, Spanish regulation has enacted Law 15/1999 on Data Protection Act (de Protección de Datos Personales). Its main purpose is 'the protection of 'people's freedom and fundamental rights, especially their right to reputation and the right to privacy' [Article 1].

105. Five significant elements can be pointed out in this Data Protection Act, 1999:

(1) The data protection principles [Article 4 to 12];

(2) The citizen rights [Article 13 to 19], within: the right to access to personal data, from anywhere; the right to know; the right to correct data; and the right to delete data.
(3) The regulation of any kind of files [Article 20 to 33].
(4) The creation of the Data Protection Agency (Agencia de Protección de Datos) [Article 35 to 42].
(5) Infractions and sanctions [Article 43 to 49].

106. The Data Protection Act, 1999, intends to balance the right to reputation and privacy on the one hand, and the requirements of the state and public authorities – governments, police, social security, the treasury of income tax departments, etc. – as well companies, on the other. It tries to guarantee fundamental rights when there is some 'necessary use' or 'interested use'. There are three principles which help in this balance:

(1) The principle of quality of data: this means not only that the personal data included must be true, but also that this data can only be held for a temporary period.
(2) The right to information when the data is requested by people.
(3) The principle of assumed consent given to anyone who requests access to the data.

2. *A New Constitutional Right to Self-Informative Determination*

107. The Constitutional Courts go beyond Ley 15/1999 on Data Protection Act (de Protección de Datos Personales). Following its own arguments in three resolutions dealing with data protection, the Constitutional Court has recognized a right related to privacy and the protection of personal data but, at the same time, much more focused on personal identity. The first case was the denial of information from a regional institution – '"Gobierno Civil", which at that time was a representative of the central government – to a citizen who was asking about their personal data as supposedly held by the "Gobierno Civil" [STC 254/1993]. The second case was the denial by a bank of the request made by an employee to delete their medical records from the database of this bank [STC 202/1999]. The third case was the constitutional procedure against articles of the Law 15/1999 on Data Protection Act (de Protección de Datos personales) [STC 292/2000].

108. The Constitutional Court states that the protection of personal data: '…is an answer to one new threat against human dignity and personal rights (…); and also, it is, by itself, a new right or a new fundamental freedom' [STC 292/2000, Fundamento jurídico 4].

109. This right is different from the 'right to privacy, art. 18.1 CE, with which it shares the aim of an efficient protection to privacy' [STC 292/2000, Fundamento jurídico 6]. The peculiarity of the right of protection of personal data lies in its different function, which is a safeguard for any individual on the power of disposition over their personal data, and at a more fundamental level, their privacy. [cf. STC 292/2000, Fundamento jurídico 6].

110. The Constitutional Court states precisely about the subject of the right of data protection: 'The object of the fundamental right of personal data protection is not only the privacy – the individual intimate data – but any kind of personal data, even if it is not intimate, when the knowledge or the use of this data by a third party can diminish the rights of a particular person. It doesn't matter if the rights concerned are or are not fundamental, because the object (of the right of personal data protection) is not only the individual intimacy – for that purpose there is the protection of art. 18.1 CE – but the personal data. Therefore, this right has to do also with the personal data which is public and accessible to anyone. But even here, the right of the protection of personal data must be efficient.' [STC 292/2000, Fundamento jurídico 6].

111. As a consequence, the protection of personal data goes beyond the right to privacy: '...the data protected (by the right of protection of personal data) is all that which identifies or allows the identification of one person; it can be ideological data, sexual, religious, economic data or any type; (the collection of this data and its manipulation) in particular circumstances can constitute a threat to individuals'. [Cf. STC 292/2000, Fundamento jurídico 6].

112. The protection of personal data thus consists mainly of: '...the prerogative to dispose of, and to control personal data means that every person has the faculty to decide which parts of their data can be transferred to a third party; it doesn't matter if this third party is the state or an individual; or which personal data can be collected by this third party. At the same time, this right allows a person to know who has access to their personal data and for what purpose. Therefore, they can oppose this possession or use.' [STC 292/2000, Fundamento jurídico 6].

113. It is precisely in this point that the right of informative self-determination connects with the right to be forgotten, a right recently recognized. Both rights can be defined as versions of the right to privacy, as adjusted to the information society.

H. Hate Speech

114. Since the 1995 Criminal Code was enacted, hate speech has been considered a crime in Spain. Article 510.1 'Those who promote discrimination, hate or violence against groups or associations, based on race, anti-Semitism or other reasons related to ideology, religion or beliefs, family situation, belonging to a particular ethnic group or race, national origin, sex, sexual orientation, disorder or disability, shall be punished with one to three years of imprisonment and six to twelve months of fine.'

115. 'The same punishment shall be applied to those who disseminate defamatory information about groups or associations in relation to their ideology, religion or beliefs, belonging to a particular ethnic group or race, national origin, sex, sexual orientation, disorder or disability, though the disseminators are aware this information is false or have a reckless disregard for the truth.'

116. The 2015 reform of the Criminal Code introduced a range of new offences related to hate speech, such as actions entailing humiliation or discredit of a group or against a certain person for belonging to such a group, for reasons of racism, anti-Semitism or others reasons; as well as the production, distribution of texts or contents through any medium that harm the dignity of persons 'because they represent serious humiliation, disregard or discredit of any of the aforementioned groups, or part thereof, or of a certain person for belonging to such a group' (Article 510.2.).

1. Protection of Children

117. Children are granted twofold legal protection in the media. First, protection is provided when children are the protagonists of TV news and entertainment programmes; in these cases, protection is aimed at their privacy and ensuring they grow up in a harmonious environment. Second, children are protected as a special audience of TV programmes and audiovisual advertising. In this area, Law 7/2010 on Audiovisual Communication is very clear on subjects, such as pornography, violence and advertising, offering a range of measures protecting children on these subjects.

Part I. Freedom of Speech

§1. Press and Broadcasting Constitutional Protection

118. Freedom of Speech in Spain contents two different rights: freedom of expression – the right to say, to express or to broadcast by any way – any opinion, thought or judgment; and the right to information, understood as the universal right to knowledge of relevant facts and opinions which contribute to the general debate in society. As the Constitution of 1978 states in the Article 20.1 a) and d) (these rights) 'are recognised and protected: the right to freely express and spread thoughts, ideas and opinions through words, in writing or by any other means of reproduction (…and) the right to freely communicate or receive truthful information by any means of dissemination whatsoever. The law shall regulate the right to the clause of conscience[9] and professional secrecy in the exercise of these freedoms'.

119. The Constitutional Court throughout the last thirty-five years of jurisprudence has shaped the meaning of freedom of expression and right to information thanks to more than 300 decisions. Its main argumentations can be gathered around four subjects: (1) the distinction between freedom of expression and right to information; (2) the balance between rights in conflict; (3) the 'Neutral Report' theory; (4) accuracy in news.

A. Freedom of Expression and Right to Information: Two Different Rights

120. It is rather unclear whether the text of the Article 20 of the Constitution distinguishes between freedom of expression [Article 20.1. a)] and right to information [Article 20.1. d)] as different rights. During the period comprising 1979–1987 even the Constitutional Court has been ambivalent about this matter. In fact, only after 1988, particularly after the sentences STC 6/1988 and STC 107/1988, the difference between freedom of expression and the right to information became clear:

> (…) in the Constitution, freedom of expression has the object of thoughts, ideas and opinions, a wide concept in which must be included beliefs and judgments too. Instead of that, (the right to information is) the right to freely communicate and to receive accurate information of facts, or, maybe more restrictively, about facts which can be considered publishable as news [Fundamento jurídico 5, STC 6/1988].

9. *See* Part II. Chapter 2. Journalists' Rights.

> (…) the distinction between thoughts, ideas and opinions on the one hand and informative communication of facts on the other (…) has a decisive importance at the time of setting the legitimacy in the exercise of these rights, therefore, meanwhile facts are subject of proof, thoughts, ideas, opinions and judgments are not subject to a demonstration of their exactitude, just because of their abstract nature, and that makes that it was not required the prove for truth or for having applied proper diligence in its inquiry (…) consequently, freedom of expression is wider than the right of information (…). [Fundamento jurídico 2, STC 107/1988].

121. After these two decisions of the Constitutional Court, the distinction between freedom of expression and right of information has been confirmed not only among the resolutions of that Court, but even in the Supreme Court and in regional courts as well. Freedom of expression has many aspects in common with the right to information; but probably the main difference among them lies in the specific reference to journalistic facts and opinions in the case of the right to information, and in the variety of forms of expression integrating the right of expression which has nothing to do with journalism. Paintings, theatrical arts, films, poetry, public religious celebrations – as the Easter week parades – all of them are embedded in the broad concept of freedom of expression.

1. The Balance Between Rights in Conflict

122. The Constitutional Court decisions show that there are some essential criteria in the substantial task of balancing rights: the accuracy of facts and the presence of public interest. As the Court insists in many of its resolutions:

> '(it is decisive) that the information spread by media was "true" – as the art. 20 1.d) CE says recognizing this right (right of information) – as well that the issues with which the information is related were in the general interest, attending both, the subject of that information and the people concerning the information'. [STC 219/1992, Fundamento jurídico 2, STC 240/1992, Fundamento jurídico 3; STC 172/1990, Fundamento jurídico 2, STC 190/11996, Fundamento jurídico 2 among others].

123. In the end, it is a matter of finding a balance between the present interests in each case. The core element for this balance is proportionality. That means: the intensity of the public interest in the knowledge of some fact can justify only certain infringements to the other's right, but never in such way that it supposes a complete abolition of that personal right. Proportionality must be applied. This proportionality can be identified with rationality, in the sense of reasonable limitation or reasonable restriction to a constitutional right. Therefore, any journalistic work which could be classified as abusive or excessive would be in opposition to the Article 20.

2. *The 'Neutral Report' Idea*

124. The 'Neutral Report' idea has been imported from American Supreme Court Case Law on freedom of expression. In fact, it is the easier argumentative solution for many conflicts caused by the quotation of somebody's report. It is quite usual that journalists refer in their articles, interviews or reports, to information already published or broadcasted by different media. Concerning these situations, the Constitutional Court has two set of conditions in order to determine whether we actually are facing a 'neutral report': (a) the clear identification of the author of the original news or opinions; (b) a clear distance must be done between the journalist and the statements said by the precedent journalist or media:

> when a Media just copy, things said or written by a third one, publishing or broadcasting exactly its transcription, then it acts not only as a media transmitting a third one's opinions or information, but also this Media is exercising it right of freely communicate accurate information, precisely trough this copy of other's statement [Fundamento jurídico 4, STC 134/1999].

125. Sometimes, the difficulty of producing a 'neutral report' lies in the degree of identification/independence from the part of the journalist, particularly in Radio and TV live programmes. Especially in the case of interviews, when the spontaneity of the journalists can easily be understood as an identification with the positions adopted by the guest of the programme. A good example was the constitutional resolution on a successful TV programme in 2007, 'Quién sabe dónde'. The journalist, Paco Lobatón, was interviewing two relatives of a missing woman. The way he conducted the interview was understood by the Court as an additive to the accusation of murder that the two women said against the missed woman's husband:

> 'the tone of the introduction, the judgments over the information, the qualification made for the protagonists, the general context and the statements pronounced, together became an amplifier tool for a concrete message assumed and presented by the TV as its own message' [Fundamento jurídico 3 y 11, STC 139, 2007].

3. *Accuracy for News*

126. Accuracy is probably one of the most valuable characteristic in the exercise of journalism. There is not a profession which speaks out more about accuracy, truth and the rest of synonyms than journalism. But which is exactly the meaning of accuracy under the Article 20, Spanish Constitution?

127. In the opinion of the Constitutional Court, accuracy applied to news is not the same as 'undoubted reality of facts' [Fundamento jurídico 3, STC 41/1994, STC 154/1999 and STC 121/2002]. The 'aim of accuracy is not the full concordance between the spread of information and the objective truth of the facts' [Fundamento jurídico 6 STC 143/1991, Fundamento jurídico 4, STC 144/1998] or just 'objectivity' [Fundamento jurídico 5, STC 154/1999]. The constitutional requirement for accuracy consists in:

> 'asking a journalist for the specific professional duty of diligence, just looking at the truth in the news or revising if a sufficient checking over the information has been done, in the way that just things transmitted as facts or news have previously been checked with objective data coming from relevant sources' [Fundamento jurídico 4, STC 144/1998].

128. But, which is exactly the meaning of 'specific professional duty of diligence'? Again, the Constitutional Court offers some light on this matter:

> 'the requirement of truth must be understood as fulfilled in these cases whereas, previously to the circulation of the news, the journalist has apply an activity of investigation over the facts with public interest, and when that investigation has been made with the level of diligence required of a journalist' 'the requirement of truth must be understood to be fulfilled in these cases, provided that, prior to circulation of the news, the journalist has performed the activity of investigation of the facts of public interest, and the investigation has been performed with the level of diligence required of a journalist' [Fundamento jurídico 3, STC 1/2005, STC 69/2006 y STC 68/2008].

129. Once this correlation between accurate information and journalists' activity is admitted, it is necessary to set some criteria in order to be applied to any journalistic work, as a standard of quality for investigating, writing and broadcasting news.

130. The doubt comes when the Constitutional Court insists many times on the concept of 'diligence' but without establishing at the same time the concrete edge between a journalist's diligence and carelessness. The only delimitation made by the Court is the definition of negligence, that it is said to be equivalent 'to transmitting as true facts just simple rumours, without making any contrast, or just simple inventions or insidious insinuations' [Cf. STC 105/1983, STC 6/1988, STC 171/1990, STC 172/1990, STC 123/1993 & STC 22/1995].

131. Accurate information is alike 'checked information with the standards of professional journalism'. And that must happen independently of the subjective intention of the journalist, because even the way he talks or the way in which he focuses the news are indifferent for the quality of accuracy [Cf. Fundamento jurídico 6 STC 192/1999, & Fundamento jurídico 4, STC 29/ 2009].

B. An Absolute Prohibition of Censorship

132. As a reaction against Franco's dictatorship era, the Constitution of 1978 (General Franco died in 1975) includes an absolute prohibition of censorship in Article 20.2. 'The exercise of these rights may not be restricted by any form of prior censorship.'

133. At the same time, Article 20.5 considers the judicial seizure of both publications and taping programmes: 'The seizure of publications, recordings and other means of information may only be carried out by means of a court order.' In this sense, Article 20.5 complements the reference to the prohibited censorship: Article 20.5.

134. It is true that, in some cases, the practical application of this Article 20.5 can produce the same effects as censorship – as a prior prohibition for printing or broadcasting, but the reference to Court changes everything. Because it is not only the arbitrary decision which comes from a governmental department, without any guarantee of fairness, but the judicial order coming from an independent institution as the Judicial Power is. One representative case which illustrates this idea is the *'Máquina de la verdad' v. Telecinco-Gestevisión* case.

135. The Constitutional Court has known about the '*Máquina de la verdad*' case in 1999, STC 187/1999. La 'Máquina de la verdad' had been a TV show very successful in the 1990s in Spain. It was about trying to probe the truth of a story, usually a controversial story that had been placed in frontlines of media, or at least in some yellow magazines. The core of the TV show is the use of a lie detector with the main protagonists of the selected story. Julián Lago, a famous Spanish journalist was the conductor of that TV programme of Telecinco (Commercial TV), in 1993. In that case, the Constitutional Court had to decide if the decision made by the judge concerning the provisional prohibition of broadcast one particular programme was justified or not by the Constitution (during the days 16 and 27December 1993 and 1 February 1994). According to the opinion of Telecinco-Gestevisión, the judicial seizure in this case is equivalent to censorship which is absolutely prohibited by the Article 20.2 of the Constitution. The main reason sustained by Telecinco-Gestevisión in that sense was that the entire activity of the judicial institution had been just verifying in advance the content of such information, in order to determine whether it had to be broadcasted or whether it had not, which is equivalent to prior censorship.

136. The first argumentation given by the Spanish Constitutional Court was that this prior measure, which runs in such exceptional way from the law and which consists particularly in the prohibition to broadcast this 'La Máquina de la verdad' programme, was based on the high probability that this programme's delivery could cause damage [Fundamento jurídico 2]. The Judge's decision was based on the need to protect the privacy of the accuser (couple Lecquio-Obregón) and in the consideration that this TV programme interfered in the judicial investigation over the case, because a parallel trial in Media could happen. Even if the limitation to the defendant's freedom of expression is quite evident, it is unavoidable to think of the damages that its broadcasting could have produced to the honour and the privacy of these celebrities. Particularly when a previous interview has been run by the popular magazine 'Pronto', and therefore another trial on privacy with the same protagonists and the same offences had taken place. In fact, the commercial just announcing the TV programme 'La Máquina de la Verdad' said that it was going to reveal many aspects of the couples private lives. [Fundamento jurídico 13].

137. In the opinion of the Constitutional Court, the Judge – with the elements he had access to, at that time – had made a prudential balance between rights and values, goods and rights in conflict. He presumed that, in continuity with the advertising of the TV programme, it was quite coherent that the main source of the programme – the nanny of these celebrities – would have repeated the same information, data, facts and opinions that, in fact, were under judicial investigation.

138. The dilemma about whether the requiring of the tape – made by the Judge to Telecinco – was or was not censorship, is solved – in opinion of the Constitutional

Court – through the checking of the Judge's aim on that: was it to examine the audiovisual content in order to prohibit its broadcasting or rather was the examination intended to assure just the legality of its broadcasting? Because, for the Constitutional Court, the main intentionality of the judge's requirement was this last one. Therefore, no censorship was applied [Fundamento jurídico 14].

Part II. Regulation of Print Media

Chapter 1. The Profession of Journalist

139. There are no special rules or specific conditions required to apply for work as a journalist. However, over the last twenty years, most newspaper companies have tended to hire graduates from university journalism schools and schools of communication.

140. Bloggers are not considered journalism professionals. Like other individual actors on the Internet, bloggers have the legal liability of any citizen. Bloggers therefore do not have the professional right to confidential sources or the clause of conscience granted to journalists.

Chapter 2. Journalists' Rights

§1. Role of Journalists as Watch-Dogs of Society

141. The Constitutional Court established a specific interpretation for the role of journalists with regard to the freedom of expression and the right to information. It was not exactly the same as being a watchdog of the democratic system, as mentioned in European Court of Human Rights jurisprudence, but it reinforced the concept freedom of expression and the right to information through the professional exercise of these rights in order to enable others to exercise them. The Spanish Constitutional Court based its conclusions on two main arguments. On the one hand, the social aspect of freedom of expression and the right to information depends mainly on the activities of journalists:

> 'The possibility of the free exercise of the fundamental rights of freedom of expression and information guarantees the formation and existence of free public opinion, because, given (that the possibility of the free exercise of rights) is a prior and necessary condition for the exercise of other rights inherent to a dynamic democratic system, it becomes, at the same time, one of the pillars of a free and democratic society' [Supreme Court Decision STC 52/2002, Legal Argument 4, Supreme Court Decision STC 159/1986, Legal Argument 6; 21/2000, Legal Argument 4].

142. On the other hand, a journalist is essentially somebody who helps citizens exercise their right to information as well as their freedom of expression. Professional dedication to this job places journalism and, therefore, journalists, in this deeper relationship with these fundamental rights and with citizens. One of the most meaningful traces of this special position of the profession of journalism is the conceptual correspondence between the accuracy of news, as established in Article 20 of the Constitution, and the requirement that news research, preparation and dissemination be performed with 'professional diligence', as is frequently mentioned in constitutional court jurisprudence. This 'professional diligence' is exclusively linked to journalists:

> 'the requirement of truth must be understood to be fulfilled in these cases, provided that, prior to circulation of the news, the journalist has performed the activity of investigation of the facts of public interest, and the investigation has been performed with the level of diligence required of a journalist' [Legal Argument 3, Supreme Court Decision STC 1/2005, Supreme Court Decision STC 69/2006 and Supreme Court Decision STC 68/2008].

§2. Journalists' Independence

143. Law 2/1997 on the Clause of Conscience (*Ley Orgánica 2/1997, de Cláusula de Conciencia)* implements the constitutional mandate on the matter in Article 20 of the Constitution of 1978. The Spanish law focuses on the clause of conscience, an exclusive right of journalists, by extending the scope of the clause of conscience to include some cases that are closer to objections of conscience. Strictly speaking, the clause of conscience implies: (a) the journalist concerned is an employee, and (b) the journalist resigns from his or her position in the company because performing the job causes a conflict of conscience. However, Law 2/1997 introduced the possibility of acting on one's own conscience without the need for resigning. It may be a more realistic option, given the difficulties of journalists in the area of professional rights. Regardless of whether the clause of conscience offers a solution to resigning over a labour conflict between the company and the journalist, the objection of conscience provides a softer solution for daily ethical conflicts.

144. The right to the clause of conscience grants journalists the right to leave their jobs in any media when any of the following circumstances occurs:

(a) a change in ideology of the newspaper, TV news programme or radio station;
(b) a change in the news trend of the newspaper, radio station or TV programme;
(c) a structural transformation in the media outlet that involves transferring a specific journalist to a different position in the company;
(d) when any of these new circumstances can be proved, the journalist may leave his or her job while retaining the right to receive the payment awarded in cases of wrongful dismissal.

Article 2.1. Thanks to the clause of conscience, information professionals have the right to request that the legal contract with their employer be cancelled:

(1) when an essential change (in terms of either orientation or ideology) occurs in the media outlet with which the journalist has an employment contract;
(2) when the employer decides to transfer the journalist to another media outlet within the same company if that represents a clear break with the journalist's professional orientation.

(...)

> Article 3. If reasons exist, information professionals may choose not to participate in the preparation of information that represents a conflict with the ethical principles of journalism, and they may not be penalized in any way for such a choice.

145. One of the paradoxical conditions of the Spanish media law system is that prison and special suspension penalties are applied as punishment in some cases of defamation and acts against privacy, when they occur through the media or by people related to the media, whereas freedom of expression and information are recognized as fundamental rights by the Constitution. This would also appear to be in clear contradiction with the jurisprudence of the European Court of Human Rights (mainly the case *Cumpana y Mazare v. Rumania*, 2004), which concludes that these kinds of measures can have a chilling effect on journalists. In fact, the punishments established in the Criminal Code are:

(a) a penalty of imprisonment for 6 months to two years or a fine of 6 to 24 months in the case of defamation or slander, when perpetrated through the media [cf. Article 212]
(b) a special suspension penalty of 6 months to two years in the case of defamation or slander, when performed in exchange for a price, promise or award [cf. Article 213]. This special suspension penalty involves a prohibition to work in any professional activity related to the way the crime was committed; in the case of journalists, this means a prohibition to work in any way for newspapers, radio, TV news programs, etc. [Article 45, Criminal Code].

146. For crimes against privacy in cases involving journalism and the media, the Criminal Code stipulates:

(a) One to four years of imprisonment or a fine of 12-24 months for those who, in order to discover secrets or invade the other's privacy without his/her consent, seize papers, letters, electronic mail texts or any other document or personal belongings, or use electronic devices to listen to, tape or play sounds, images or any other sign of communication [cf. Article 197.1].
(b) One to four years of imprisonment or a fine of 12-24 months for those who, without any authorisation, seize, use or modify, with damage to a third party, personal data registered in files or electronic or digital devices, or in any kind of public or private register [cf. Article 197.2].
(c) One to four years of imprisonment or a fine of 12-24 months for those who, without any permission, gain access to that information, and those who exchange or use that information to cause damage to the legitimate owner of the data or a third party [cf. Article 197.3].
(d) Two to five years of imprisonment if the information, facts discovered and images related to this information or facts are disclosed, revealed or transferred to a third party [cf. Article 197.4].

§3. Protection of Journalistic Sources

147. The only legal reference to the confidentiality of sources is in Article 20 of the Constitution of 1978:

Article 20. 1. The following rights are recognised and protected:

(…)

d) the right to freely communicate or receive truthful information by any means of dissemination whatsoever. The law shall regulate the right to the clause of conscience and professional secrecy in the exercise of these freedoms.

148. Confidentiality of sources is therefore mainly regulated by common professional rules of journalism, which are respected by judges and different authorities.

Chapter 3. Journalists' Liability

149. The only reference to a special liability regime for journalists is the subsidiary accountability for criminal offences set out in Article 30 of the Criminal Code:

Article 30.

(a) In felonies and misdemeanors that are committed using media or supports of mechanical diffusion, neither the accessories, nor those who have personally or actually favoured these shall be held criminally accountable.
(b) The principals (...) shall be held accountable in a progressive, excluding and subsidiary manner, in the following order:

1°. Those who materially drafted the text or produced the sign concerned, and those who induced others to perpetrate the act;

2°. The directors of the publication or program in which it is disseminated;

3°. The directors of the printing, broadcasting or distribution company;

4°. The directors of the recording, playing or printing company.

150. The purpose of this kind of regulation is to guarantee that somebody is going to take the control of the content of media, at least under the pressure of having a possible criminal responsibility.

Chapter 4. Right to Reply

151. The right of reply is recognized in regulation – Organic Act 2/1984 on Rectification – for any media – press, radio, TV, Internet.

§1. Subject

152. The right of rectification or right of reply can be exercised by any natural or legal person, whether directly or through his or her representatives or heirs should the wronged party be deceased (Article 1).

153. The obligation to conduct the rectification lies with the director of the medium where the inaccurate or incomplete information has been disclosed.

§2. Scope of the Action of Rectification

154. Rectification under the terms established by the law is applied to all media, private and public, and for the latter the following provisions shall apply:

> Article 7. 'The claim prior to the judicial phase shall not be necessary when the information subject to the rectification being claimed has been published or disseminated through a public medium of communication'.

§3. Conditions for Rectification

155. The Organic Act establishes five requirements for a rectification to be conducted. Article 1. 'Any natural or legal person is entitled to the right of rectification of information disseminated by any social media where the former is involved which is deemed to be inaccurate and the dissemination of which can lead to his or her detriment.' As a result:

156. 1) only information on facts can be rectified. We must admit that sometimes it is hard to tell when information constitutes a fact or an opinion, since the way of telling the news, the approach to them or even the fact that a piece of news has been selected among many others indicates in many cases the subjective opinion of the informing party. However, the law emphasizes the fact that intervention is only possible when the information concerns facts.

157. 2) The facts must involve a natural or legal person, without the need for such to be expressly mentioned by name. It shall be sufficient for there to be hints leading to his/her identification.

158. 3) Rectification shall apply if the concerned facts are false or the affected party considers them to be inaccurate. A subjective approach to them shall justify the action for rectification.

159. 4). The dissemination of such information on facts can be detrimental to the affected party.

160. 5) The information has been indeed disseminated through a medium.

§4. Procedure for Rectification

161. This can be a two-phase procedure. In the first phase, the affected party addresses the director of the medium for the rectification to be conducted (Article 2). When the affected party can prove that this first step has been unsuccessful – either because the rectification has not been made or because it has been insufficient – the second phase before a judge is initiated (Article 4).

§5. The Phase Before the Director of the Medium

162. The person seeking rectification must submit a rectification request in writing to the director of the medium, its contents addressing only the facts of the information intended to be rectified and with a similar length to such. It shall be submitted within seven days after the information is disseminated.

163. If the director of the medium decides to publish the rectification, it shall be published in full within a period of three days since the rectification request letter was received, unless the periodicity of the medium were different, in which case the rectification should adapt to such. The rectification shall be published free of charge, without adding any comments or notes and with a similar relevance to that given to the allegedly inaccurate information.

§6. The Judicial Phase

164. The judicial phase can be initiated after seven working days from the date when the rectification should have been made public. No solicitor or '*procurador*' is required to intervene in this phase. The affected party shall submit to the first instance judge – whether that assigned to the affected party's address or to that assigned to the registered office of the medium – a writ indicating the rectification seeking to be published, proof that it has been submitted to the medium within the adequate period and, to the extent possible, the information wished to be rectified. The judge then decides whether to admit or dismiss the action for rectification in respect of the writ and issues a decision.

165. If action for rectification is admitted, the procedure to issue a decision is as follows:

(a) the rectification seeker and the director of the medium – or their representatives – are summoned to attend an oral hearing within a period of seven days after admission of the claim;

(b) during the oral hearing, the judge shall only admit pertinent evidence which the parties can present during the act;
(c) the decision shall be issued on the same date as the oral hearing or the day after at the latest;
(d) the decision shall only concern the rejection of the claim or order to conduct the rectification;
(e) the judge orders the payment of the costs of procedures to the party whose petition has been dismissed (article 6: '(...) shall order the payment of the costs of proceedings to the party whose petitions have been rejected in full')

166. This action for rectification shall be compatible with the exercise of criminal or civil action concerning the same facts. Another peculiarity of the procedure for rectification is that, even though appeals can be brought against first instance decisions, if the ruling were challenged by means of an appeal, the execution of the decision would not be prevented, meaning that the medium shall publish the rectification within three days upon the ruling.

167. The goal of the right of reply, as regulated in Spain, is to prevent damages from occurring as a result of the dissemination of information, irrespective of the fact of such information being true or false, as these terms shall only be verified by means of civil or criminal proceedings.

Chapter 5. Access to Public Information

168. Act 19/2013, of 9 December, on Transparency, Access to Information and Good Governance stems from the principle that:

> 'Transparency, access to public information and standards for good governance shall be the cornerstones of any political action. Only when the actions of public decision-makers are scrutinised, when citizens can know how the decisions that affect them are made, how public funds are handled or which criteria underlie the actions undertaken by our public institutions, we will be witnessing the start of a process in which public authorities begin to answer the questions of a critical, demanding society that requires participation in public power' (preamble to the Act).

169. On the one hand, this regulation enhances transparency in public activity as it establishes obligations for all public bodies in this regard. On the other hand, it ensures the right of access to information, in line with the Spanish Constitution of 1978 which so states in Article 105b). In addition, it establishes the legal obligation to make a 'Transparency Portal' available to offer citizens the most relevant and updated data regarding the public administration in office (Article 7). The limitations applicable to the right of access to public information result from the damage such could cause to (Article 14.1.):

(1) National security.
(2) Defence.
(3) External relationships.
(4) Public safety.
(5) The prevention, investigation and penalization of criminal, administrative or disciplinary offences.
(6) Equality between the parties during legal proceedings and effective legal protection.
(7) The administrative tasks for vigilance, inspection and control.
(8) Economic and commercial interests.
(9) Economic and monetary policies.
(10) Professional secrecy and intellectual and industrial property.
(11) The guarantee of confidentiality or secrecy required in decision-making processes.
(12) Environmental protection.

Chapter 6. Press Council

170. There is no equivalent to the Press Council in Spain. A relevant representation of the press is the Federación de las Asociaciones de Periodistas Españoles (Federation of Spanish Journalist Associations, or FAPE) created in 1992. It mostly focuses on organizing activities for journalists in practise and on giving their opinion on journalism-related controversies that will serve as institutional representation.

Part III. Regulation of Audiovisual Media (Broadcasting)

Chapter 1. Public Service Broadcasting

§1. The Concept and Mission of Public Service Broadcasting

171. According to General Law 7/2010 on Audiovisual Media (Ley General de la Comunicación Audiovisual), the public audiovisual media service is an essential service of general economic interest. The state, autonomous communities (Spanish regions) and local entities are allowed to provide public audiovisual media services with the aim of broadcasting free-to-air general or special-interest channels, excluding channels dedicated exclusively to commercial broadcasting.

172. Article 40 of this law states that the mission of this public audiovisual media service is to broadcast content that promotes constitutional principles and values, to contribute to the formation of diverse public opinion, to raise awareness about Spain's cultural and linguistic diversity, to disseminate knowledge and the arts, with a special emphasis on the promotion of an audiovisual culture, and to address the needs of minority citizens and social groups. To achieve this, the public audiovisual media service must produce, edit and broadcast a set of radio, television and online news service channels with diverse and balanced scheduling for all audience types and covering all genres, with a view to meeting society's need for information, culture, education and entertainment and preserving pluralism in the media.

173. In addition to these general obligations for all public, state, regional and local operators, the state-owned operator, Spanish Radio and Television Corporation (RTVE) must assume an initial set of general obligations that are stipulated in Law 17/2006, of 5 June, on State-Owned Radio and Television, and a further set of more specific obligations, which are set out in General Law 7/2010, on Audiovisual Media. With respect to the more general obligations, Law 17/2006 stipulates that RTVE must:

(a) Promote the dissemination and knowledge of constitutional principles and civic values.
(b) Guarantee objective, accurate and plural information; it must comply with the criteria of professional independence and political, social and ideological pluralism that exists in society; and it must clearly distinguish between fact and opinion.

(c) Facilitate democratic discussion and freedom of expression.
(d) Promote democratic participation by guaranteeing the right to access.
(e) Promote territorial cohesion and the linguistic and cultural plurality and diversity of Spain.
(f) Promote the exchange of information and mutual understanding between the citizens of the member states of the European Union, as an area of co-existence.
(g) Edit and broadcast radio and television channels with international coverage to help raise awareness of Spanish languages and cultures abroad and to meet the needs of Spanish nationals residing or displaced abroad.
(h) Provide access to different program genres and institutional, social, cultural and sporting events for all audience sectors, with a special focus on topics of special public interest.
(i) Promote the dissemination and knowledge of Spanish cultural productions, especially audiovisual productions.
(j) Support the social integration of minorities and target social groups with specific needs.
(k) Promote the protection and safeguarding of equality between men and women and avoid all discrimination between the sexes.
(l) Promote knowledge of the arts, science, history and culture.
(m) Disseminate knowledge of consumer and user rights, and develop procedures to guarantee the right of reply.
(n) Encourage the production of European audiovisual content and Spanish-language audiovisual content, and promote digital and multimedia creation as a contribution to the development of Spanish and European cultural industries.
(o) Monitor the preservation of historic audiovisual files.
(p) Address the widest possible audience and ensure maximum continuity and geographic and social coverage, with a commitment to offering quality, diversity and innovation while complying with ethical requirements.
(q) Promote the values of peace.
(r) Promote knowledge, safeguard and respect ecological values, and protect the environment.
(s) Protect the rights of minors.
(t) Contribute to the development of the information society.

174. In terms of the more specific obligations, these are detailed in section 9 of General Law 7/2010 of 31 March on Audiovisual Media. The first is to ensure the right of access by dedicating at least twelve hours a week, not during graveyard slots, through any of its different radio and television channels, to broadcasting programmes and incorporating interactive services that represent political, trade union and social groups. It must also periodically report on parliamentary debates in the Spanish parliament and transmit live broadcasts of sessions of special public interest on the radio, television and Internet and of electoral debates during elections. With regard to children's programmes, 30% of the programmes on the children's channel that are broadcast on weekdays between 17:00 and 21:00 local time must be aimed at children between the ages of 4 and 12. At weekends and on public holidays, this obligation shall apply between 9:00 and 21:00 local time and must make use of the multilingual system, which should feature, as a minimum, Spanish, co-official languages of the state and English, provided that it has the technical means and financial resources to do so. This scheduling shall increase progressively until European programmes represent the majority of children's programmes.

175. With respect to access for people with disabilities, it is required to subtitle 90% of its programmes, with a view to eventually subtitling 100%, provided that it has the technical means to do so, and to broadcast at least ten hours a week of programmes with sign language and a further ten hours with audio descriptions. With regard to European production quotas, RTVE must screen at least 60% of its feature films and short films, films made for television, documentaries, series and news, cultural and topical programmes produced by the European audiovisual industry during peak time slots on its main channels. In addition, it must increase its legal investment in the funding of European feature films, short films, films, documentaries and animation products by 20%. It is required to promote independent production by diversifying the contracting of external services and outside or mixed productions; one sole supplier may not exceed 30% of the total, except for companies with significant market power or exclusive rights holders. In order to avoid competition with private operators, RTVE may not allocate more than 10% of its total annual budget for supplies, purchases and external services to the acquisition of broadcasting rights for official sporting events classified as of general interest, except for the Olympic and Paralympic Games. Furthermore, RTVE may not broadcast, across the entirety of its channels, more than fifty-two film premières produced by major international film production companies a year at peak times.

176. It must promote culture and art, scientific and technological dissemination, innovation and entrepreneurial activity, and guarantee international radio and television broadcasts with quality content that is fundamentally informative in nature and promotes culture and the strategic political and economic interests of Spain and its territories.

177. It must ensure maximum geographical, social and cultural coverage and promote cultural and linguistic diversity in its range of digital services, especially through a channel dedicated to cultural and artistic production. If it has the technical means and financial resources to do so, RTVE must acquire and broadcast audiovisual content produced in the different autonomous communities and, when such content is in a co-official language, broadcast it in a dual system alongside Spanish. Likewise, in territories with co-official languages, versions of recorded fiction, animation and documentary programmes that are dubbed into or subtitled with these languages must be broadcast, depending on each autonomous community's linguistic reality.

178. The general public service objectives are set out in a framework mandate (*mandato marco*) for a period of nine years, whereas each public service channel must have a programme contract (*contrato programa*) that explicitly identifies the public service content. Activities or content that do not comply with the public service function cannot be financed with public money. The competent audiovisual authorities must assess whether any significant new services fulfil the public service mission and whether they distort competition in the audiovisual market. In practise, this assessment has not yet been applied, since no framework mandate has so far been signed.

179. Regarding media ownership, the General Law on Audiovisual Media prohibits public administrations and public audiovisual media service providers from owning the share capital of private audiovisual media service providers. Moreover, at national level, the National Technical Plan stipulates that the state cannot reserve for or award to public audiovisual media service providers more than 25% of the available frequency spectrum for the provision of the national television service or more than 35% for national radio services.

180. The Market and Competition Commission (CNMC) is responsible for monitoring compliance with this provision and all specific regulations and standards on this subject, in terms of scheduling and content.

§2. The Organization of Public Service Broadcasting

181. The organization of public service broadcasting in Spain is complex and heterogeneous. An easy way to reduce its complexity is to view it as a reflection of the country's political structure. The Spanish executive branch has three levels: local, regional and state. The public service media replicates these three levels. Given the wide variety of situations, this section will focus solely on the organization, structure and functioning of the state-level operator, RTVE, which is the most important in terms of audience and the only operator that covers the entire country.

182. The organization and structure of RTVE is regulated by Law 17/2006, of 5 June, on State-Owned Radio and Television. This law grants the management of the state-level public radio and television service to RTVE. The corporation is set up as a public limited company subject to commercial legislation. RTVE is directed and governed by the Board of Directors, whose chairperson presides over the board and the ordinary executive directorate. To better fulfil the public service mission, an Advisory Committee and an Information Committee have been created. RTVE's Board of Directors is composed of nine members who must have, by law, sufficient qualifications and professional experience; specifically, they will have performed administrative, senior management, control, advisory or similar functions in a public or private entity for a term of not less than five years or possess relevant qualifications in the field of communication or professional, teaching or research experience.

183. The resolutions of the Board of Directors are adopted by a majority of its members, who are elected by the Spanish Parliament: five by the Congress of Deputies and four by the Senate. The proposed candidates must appear at a public hearing in Congress and the Senate to verify their suitability for the position. Their election requires a two-thirds majority of the corresponding chamber, but if a two-thirds majority is not reached within twenty-four hours of the first ballot, both chambers may elect the members of the Board of Directors by absolute majority. The Congress of Deputies appoints the member who will hold the position of Chairperson of RTVE and the Board of Directors from the nine elected members.

184. The term of office of directors is six years from their appointment. This appointment is not renewable. Once the term is over, outgoing directors will continue in their functions until new directors have been appointed, a situation that has occurred frequently in recent years. To avoid coinciding with electoral cycles, the Board of Directors is partially renewed every three years, by equal quotas.

185. Members of the Board of Directors cannot be dismissed by the government, but by Congress, and a two-thirds majority is required. However, in this case there is no second absolute majority ballot as is the case with appointments. However, directors may be dismissed automatically for not complying with certain economic conditions that involve expenditure control and budgetary compliance.

186. The Advisory Committee is the body that enables society to participate in RTVE. It is made up of a total of sixteen members, who are appointed as follows:

(a) Three members by the Economic and Social Council.
(b) Two members by the Council of Consumers and Users.
(c) One member by the Ministry of Foreign Affairs and Cooperation.
(d) One member by the Spanish Youth Council.
(e) One member by the Spanish Institute for Women's Affairs.
(f) One member by the bodies representing people with disabilities.
(g) One member by the General Emigration Council.
(h) One member by the Academy of Television Arts and Sciences.
(i) One member by the Academy of Motion Picture Arts.
(j) One member by the University Coordination Council from academic experts in the fields of social science and communication.
(k) One member by the bodies representing advertisers.
(l) One member by the bodies representing journalists at state level.
(m) One director by common agreement by all trade unions involved in RTVE.

187. The functions of the Advisory Committee are to advise RTVE's Board of Directors concerning general scheduling guidelines; to provide advice regarding the criteria and rules that guarantee the right of access of significant social groups according to their social relevance, representativeness and scope of action; to provide information about proposed programme contracts with the state and scheduling areas; and to assist in the establishment of advertising admission standards. The Advisory Committee is convened by the Board of Directors at least every three months.

188. Law 17/2006 defines Information Committees as RTVE's internal participation bodies for information professionals whose aim is to monitor independence and objectivity and the veracity of the information content that is broadcast. Their main functions include ensuring the independence of information professionals from the directors of each company; promoting the editorial independence of the RTVE Corporation, in accordance with the provisions of general audiovisual legislation and this Law with respect to its public service functions; providing advice about the editorial line and news scheduling; and participating in the creation of style guides and providing non-binding advice on appointment proposals for the directors of RTVE's information services.

§3. The Financing of Public Service Broadcasting

189. The General Law on Audiovisual Media regulates spending control mechanisms for public audiovisual media services. Funding that exceeds the net cost of the public service has to be refunded or discounted from the state compensation budgeted for in the subsequent financial year. To this end, public service broadcasters must have separate accounts for each activity type, as well as an analytical accounting system that separates revenues and costs related to public service activity from those related to commercial content and other activities. They should also ensure the structural separation of their activities in order to guarantee transfer pricing and respect for market conditions. Finally, public audiovisual media service providers must not underprice their products or services or use public compensation to outbid private competitors for the right to broadcast high-value content.

A. RTVE Corporation

190. The national public service broadcaster, RTVE, is further regulated by Law 17/2006 on State-Owned Radio and Television, and Law 8/2009 on the Funding of the Spanish Radio and Television Corporation. Law 8/2009 excluded advertising as a source of income and introduced a new financial model for RTVE based on a direct subsidy from the state, plus a share, first of 80% and then of 100%, of the amount received by the state through the levy on radio spectrum use (up to a maximum of EUR 380 million) and the amount generated through two new taxes: one imposed on national telecommunications operators that provide audiovisual services (0.9% of their revenues) and another imposed on national commercial television companies that operate pay-TV or free-to-air services via cable, satellite or terrestrial networks (1.5% of the revenues of pay-TV broadcasters and 3% of the revenues of free-to-air TV broadcasters).

191. RTVE may obtain additional income from providing services to third parties, from marketing its content, and from sponsorship and the exchange of sports and cultural events for advertising purposes, provided that they fall within RTVE's public service remit.

B. Regional Public Service Broadcasting

192. Spain's public service media replicates the decentralized administrative structure of the state, which has three levels: national, regional and local. There are seventeen regions in Spain, twelve of which have a public service broadcaster. The remaining regions provide broadcasting services through private companies. Most of these regional public service broadcasters have been strongly criticized by private broadcasters and the People's Party (the current ruling party) for their inefficiency, the waste of financial resources and their abuse of public funding to the detriment of private broadcasters. Regional public service broadcasters were subject to the same general funding rules included in the General Law on Audiovisual Media, except for the prohibition of advertisements, which applies only to RTVE. However, the government deemed it necessary to further reform the legal system in 2012. An amendment to the General Law on Audiovisual Media was therefore adopted by the Spanish Parliament in July 2012, and a new legal framework for regional public service broadcasters was introduced to give regional public service broadcasters greater flexibility in the provision of their audiovisual media services (Law 6/2012, of 1 August, modifying General Law 7/2010, on Audiovisual Media, to make the models for managing regional audiovisual media services more flexible). According to this amendment, the autonomous communities may opt for direct or indirect management of their public service broadcasters through various models, including public-private partnership. If an autonomous community chooses not to provide public service broadcasting, it may issue a call for tenders to award the available licences to private service providers. Moreover, an autonomous community may transfer its public service broadcasting to a third party in accordance with specific legislation. If an autonomous community opts for an indirect management model or any other means of public-private partnership for the provision of a public audiovisual media service, then it may participate in the capital of the broadcaster providing this service. The amendment permits arrangements between regional public service broadcasters for the joint production or editing of content to improve their business efficiency. It also imposes obligations on regional public service broadcasters such as maximum expenditure limits for the financial year in question and the submission of an annual report.

Chapter 2. Private Broadcasting

§1. Different Categories of Private Broadcasters

193. The General Law on Audiovisual Media distinguishes between audiovisual media services that are provided via terrestrial airwaves and require a licence from the competent regulatory authority based on public competition, and those that are provided via means other than terrestrial airwaves (e.g., cable, satellite, IPTV and VOD), which require only prior notice to the competent regulatory authority. As with public broadcasters, there are also three geographical levels for private terrestrial broadcasters: local, regional and state.

A. Licensed Services

194. A licence provides the exclusive right to use a part of the frequency spectrum in accordance with the National Technical Plan. The state is responsible for establishing this National Technical Plan, so autonomous communities cannot launch licence tenders until the relevant part of the frequency spectrum has been planned by the state. It specifies the geographical area covered by the broadcast, the number of channels, the multiplex allocated and whether the broadcast will be free-to-air or paid for through a conditional access system. These conditions must be fulfilled, even if technological advances mean that the frequency spectrum allocated may be used more efficiently (e.g., a greater number of pay or free-to-air channels are possible). Service providers may broadcast pay-TV channels with totally or partially paid-for content, as long as the frequency spectrum used is less than or equal to 50% of the total allocated spectrum.

195. Providers must win a public tender to be awarded concession of an audiovisual licence. All available licences of the same nature and the same scope of coverage must be offered simultaneously, and upon confirmation that there is enough radio spectrum. The tender notice will specify the service provision conditions for each licence. If a maximum of six months has lapsed since the allocation of a public radio frequency and the competent administration has not requested that it be assigned to the public radio and television broadcasting service, or has not decided to assign it to the general interest media service, any interested party is entitled to propose the corresponding invitation to tender.

196. To obtain an audiovisual media licence, the following conditions must be fulfilled:

(a) In the case of individuals, being a national of a Member State of the European Economic Area or of any state that recognizes the right of Spanish nationals to hold an audiovisual licence (principle of reciprocity).

(b) In the case of bodies corporate, having a registered office in a Member State of the European Economic Area or in any state that recognizes the right of Spanish bodies corporate to hold an audiovisual licence.
(c) The licensee must have a representative who is resident in Spain, for the purposes of notifications.
(d) In the case of bodies corporate, participation in the share capital of individuals or bodies corporate from countries that are not members of the European Economic Area must also comply with the principle of reciprocity.

197. Moreover, shares in a licensee's capital held by an individual or body corporate from a country that is not a member of the European Economic Area may not exceed, directly or indirectly, 25%. Furthermore, the total shares in a licensee's capital held by individuals or bodies corporate from countries that are not members of the European Economic Area must be less than 50%.

198. Audiovisual licences are granted for a period of fifteen years. Licences are renewed automatically for the same period as initially stipulated, provided that the conditions for holding a licence are fulfilled and the service provision terms have been respected in the previous licence period, no unexpected and insurmountable technical obstacles have arisen with regard to the radio frequency in question and the service provider is up to date with payment of all fees for allocation of the public radio frequency and the fees laid down in the General Law on Audiovisual Media. Exceptionally, a licence will not be automatically renewed if the radio frequency is exhausted, one or more third parties apply for the licence at least twenty-four months before the 'licence expires and the new applicants fulfil the same conditions as those met by previous holders of the licence'.

199. Legal transactions concerning audiovisual media licences require the prior authorization of the competent audiovisual authority and are subject to payment of a fee to be determined by the government for licences with national coverage or by the autonomous communities in all other cases. Such authorization may be refused only when the applicant fails to comply with all the legal conditions for obtaining the licence or is not subrogated to the obligations of the previous licensee. In addition, licence leasing and transfer are subject to the following conditions:

(1) At least two years have passed since the licence was awarded.
(2) In the case of individuals or bodies corporate from countries that are not members of the European Economic Area, they are subject to the principle of reciprocity and payment of a fee. Exceptionally, the government or competent regional body may authorize such an operation on the grounds of public interest when the principle of reciprocity is not met. This exception must comply with the provisions of the international treaties and conventions to which Spain is party, and the competent audiovisual authority must have been consulted.
(3) No more than 50% of the licence capacity may be leased if the licence involves the award of a full multiplex or a multiplex of two or more channels. Such leasing must comply with the provisions of Article 24.3 of the General Law on Audiovisual Media concerning the use of the multiplex frequency spectrum and the use of channels with total or partial pay content (*see supra*).

(4) The leasing of channels may be authorized only if the lessee certifies compliance with all the legal conditions for obtaining the licence.
(5) Subleasing is prohibited under all circumstances.
(6) Compliance with the service requirements of the licence.

200. All audiovisual media service providers are required to register with a public national or regional registry, depending on their area of coverage. Entities with significant shares in audiovisual media service providers must also register with this registry, and indicate the percentage of capital they hold.

B. Non-linear Services

201. Until the approval of the General Law on Audiovisual Media in 2010, video-on-demand (VOD) services, near-VOD services and the transmission of information, texts, images and sound were regarded as electronic communications services and therefore subject to the regime established in General Law 32/2003 on Telecommunications and its implementing regulations. Any entity that wanted to provide these services had to fulfil the conditions established in Article 6 of the said law: due notification to the independent body, which at the time was the Telecommunications Market Commission, a description of the service to be provided, a description of the network it would operate on, etc.

202. The General Law on Audiovisual Media changed this situation. First, 'programme catalogue service providers' were defined as 'individuals or bodies corporate recognised as providers of media services in the form of on-demand audiovisual media services that, directly or indirectly, enable retail customers to view motion pictures, films made for television and television series on a fixed, portable or mobile player with IP network access'. This definition includes the obligation to reserve a minimum of 30% of their catalogue for European works, at least half of which must be in one of Spain's official languages (Article 5.2). In addition, they are required to have a technology system that provides for parental control of the content (Article 7).

203. Thus, since the General Law on Audiovisual Media was approved, VOD services have become audiovisual media services, provided that they are exercised by individuals or bodies corporate with effective control (i.e., editorial responsibility for the selection of programmes and content) and do not constitute the mere broadcast or transmission of the audiovisual programme signal. If they comply with these conditions and they operate throughout the country or in more than one autonomous community, they must be registered as on-demand video services in the CNMC's register of operators.

C. Community Audiovisual Services

204. According to Article 32 of General Law 7/2010 on Audiovisual Media, private entities that are legally regarded as non-profit making bodies may provide non-profit making community audiovisual media services in order to meet the specific social, cultural and communications needs of communities and social groups, promote citizen participation and help structure the community fabric. In any case, such content should be broadcast free-to-air and without any form of audiovisual commercial communication. However, this option is conditional upon the state being able to guarantee the availability of the public radio frequency required for the provision of such services. Since the law was approved in 2010, this availability has not been guaranteed, which means that the community audiovisual services that are broadcast in Spain today are being done so illegally, without licences. The law stipulates that the provision of such services requires a licence. This licence establishes the conditions that ensure their non-profit making character and may establish the shared use of a single channel and the conditions for such use. The awarding of the licence involves the concession for private use of the public radio frequency available for the provision of the service. The sale or lease of this licence and shifts towards commercial activity are prohibited. In addition, the entities providing these services must justify the source of their funds and provide a breakdown of their expenditure and income, if any. The audiovisual authority must establish a financial management evaluation system and a specific register for them to deposit financial reports. The economic conditions are stringent: unless expressly authorized by the audiovisual authority, annual operating costs may not exceed EUR 100,000 in the case of audiovisual television media services and EUR 50,000 in the case of radio audiovisual media services.

Chapter 3. Programme Standards

§1. Impartiality

205. General Act on Audiovisual Media 7/2010 does not expressly mention the standard of impartiality. However, it does refer to the need for a 'plurality of media, whether public, commercial and community media that reflect the ideological, political and cultural diversity of society' (Article 14.1). In this context, public audiovisual services are required to offer:

206. Article 40.1. '(…) a set of radio stations, television channels and information services in line with diverse broadcast programming, balanced for all kinds of public, covering all genres, intended to fulfil the need for information, culture, education and entertainment of society and preserve pluralism in the media'.

207. Other principles related to impartiality that are also required from audiovisual services are those of truthfulness, when applied to news, and the need to separate information from opinion: Article 5.5: 'All individuals are entitled to informative communication being conducted in compliance with the duty of care in terms of verification of the truthfulness of information and for communication to be respectful toward political, social and cultural diversity.' Article 5.6. 'All individuals are entitled to be informed of events of general interest and to receive information and opinion in a clearly separated manner.'

§2. Cultural Diversity

208. The General Act on Audiovisual Media also mentions the right of individuals for 'audiovisual media to be provided through diverse sources and contents and to the existence of different areas of coverage as per the State territory organisation' (Article 14.1). This right endorses the existence of regional and local television channels. At the same time, it points out the obligation of audiovisual media service operators, in particular public audiovisual companies, to promote the knowledge and dissemination of the languages existing within Spain and their cultural expression (Article 14.3).

209. Regarding the audience's 'right to cultural and linguistic diversity' (Article 5), the following obligations for the television media service providers are set out:

- To reserve 51% of the annual broadcasting time of each channel or set of channels of the provider to broadcast European works; out of such percentage, to reserve 50% to broadcast European titles in any of the Spanish languages. For programme catalogue providers, this obligation shall mean that they are to reserve 30% of their catalogue to European works and, out of such percentage, half shall be broadcasted in any of the languages existing in Spain.
- In any case, 10% of total broadcasting shall be reserved to independent producers, and half of said 10% must have been produced in the past five years.

- In addition, they shall contribute annually to the financing of the European production of cinematographic films, television films and series, as well as documentaries and animated films and series, with 5% of the revenue accrued during the previous financial year, as per their operating account, from those channels in which said audiovisual products are broadcast no more than seven years after their production.
- For 'national or regional coverage' public television channels, contribution shall amount to 6%. This obligation is alleviated by the possibility of such financing being provided 'as direct participation in the production of such or in the acquisition of commercial rights over such'.
- There is also the possibility to use this contribution to finance films, series and mini-series for television broadcasting (up to 40% for private channels and up to 25% for public ones, the latter also being required to use a minimum of 50% of said percentage to finance television films or mini-series).
- Local television stations not included in nationwide networks shall be exempted from these obligations.

§3. Protection of Minors (Indecency and Violence)

210. Prohibited or restricted contents. Minors are protected from pornographic and violent messages as these are deemed to be highly detrimental. Article 7.2. 'Audiovisual contents that may seriously impair the physical, mental or moral development of minors shall not be emitted, particularly those including scenes of pornography, abuse, gender violence or gratuitous violence. Any other contents that are likely to impair the physical, mental or moral development of minors shall only be broadcast in free-access television between 10 p.m. and 6 a.m. and shall always be preceded by an audio and visual warning as per the criteria established by the competent audiovisual authority. The visual warning shall remain on screen during the whole programme including such contents. When these contents are broadcast through a conditional access system, audiovisual media service providers shall include parental control systems. (…).'

A. Measures for Content Rating and to Establish Special Protection Time Slots

211. The body in charge of rating contents is the Comisión Nacional de los Mercados y la Competencia, but such ratings must be approved by the Code of Self-Regulation for Television Contents and Childhood (Código de Autorregulación de Contenidos Televisivos e Infancia). On the other hand, the competent audiovisual authority – that is, Audiovisual Councils in those regions where they exist – shall be in charge of supervising, controlling and penalizing programme ratings by television audiovisual media service providers. Article 7.6. 'All audiovisual products distributed through television audiovisual media services shall be age-rated as per the rating instructions dictated by the Consejo Estatal de Medios Audiovisuales' (National Council for Audiovisual Media).

212. Rating shall be recognized as per the Code of Self-Regulation for Television Contents and Childhood (Código de Autorregulación de Contenidos Televisivos e Infancia) 'The competent audiovisual authority shall be in charge of supervising, controlling and penalising the adequate rating of programmes by television audiovisual media service providers.'

213. In addition to this, three special protection watersheds are established to protect minors. Article 7.2. '(…) In addition, three special protection watersheds are established, taking the time zone in mainland Spain as reference: between 8 and 9 a.m. and between 5 and 8 p.m. in business days, as well as between 9 a.m. and 12 p.m. on Saturdays, Sundays and national holidays. Contents rated as not recommended for minors younger than thirteen years of age shall be emitted outside said watersheds and the age rating visual warning shall remain on screen during the whole programme. The special protection watersheds applicable to Saturdays and Sundays shall also be applicable to the following dates: 1st and 6th January, Good Friday, 1st May, 12th October, 1st November and 6th, 8th and 25th December (…).'

B. Measures That Allow Parents or Legal Guardians to Select Programmes

214. The most significant innovation among the measures to protect minors, under Article 7 of General Act on Audiovisual Media 7/2010, is the obligation for all television audiovisual media service providers – including subscription providers – to provide digital coding for all programmes as per the age rating of their contents so parental control can be exercised. Article 7.2. '(…) All television audiovisual media service providers, including non-linear services, shall use digital coding for age rating of contents to allow parental control. The coding system shall be approved by the Audiovisual Authority.'

215. Royal Decree 920/2006, of 28 July, enacting the General Regulation of Cable Television and Radio Broadcasting, establishes a similar obligation. Article 12. Protection for minors and other access measures. '1. In accordance with the fourth additional provision of Act 25/1994, of 12 July, the holders of authorisations to provide cable radio and television broadcasting services shall adopt the necessary measures, whether of a physical or virtual nature, to impede full or partial access in receivers to any of its channels at the user's discretion in an easy and comfortable manner.'

§4. Human Dignity

216. Audiovisual media services shall spread the values of respect towards dignity of human beings, as well as those rights expressing such dignity, such as right to honour, to privacy and to the protection of personal reputation. As described in General Act on Audiovisual Media 7/2010.

217. Article 4.2. 'Audiovisual media shall never incite hatred or discrimination on the account of gender or any personal or social circumstance and shall remain respectful toward human dignity and constitutional values, eradicating in particular any conducts encouraging inequality for women. (…) 4. Audiovisual media shall respect the honor, privacy and protection of personal reputation of individuals (…).'

§5. Right of Reply

218. Public television and radio laws of a national and regional scope refer to the general laws existing on the right of rectification (Act 2/1984 on Rectification) as a standard to be exercised in these media. The only exception is Act 5/1982, of 20 May, on the Creation of the Basque Public Television and Radio Body which refers to the right of reply under the following terms. Article 27.1:

> To exercise the right of reply, the authors of works of a literary, artistic, scientific or similar nature or the persons performing as professionals in public entertainment and who are mentioned or referred to by critics regarding said works or performances shall not be deemed unfairly prejudiced, as long as the critics:

(a) limit themselves to the public activity conducted by the concerned parties or to artistic or scientific assessment, and
(b) abide by the principles and rights set forth in this Act

> 2. By virtue of the guarantees of freedom of expression, any other person conducting or having conducted a public activity of any nature shall not be deemed unfairly prejudiced when mention or reference to them refers to said activity and abides by the principles and rights set forth in this Act.

Chapter 4. Political Broadcasting

§1. Rules on Political Independence of Broadcasters

219. The rules on political independence of audiovisual media service providers are set out in the General Act on Audiovisual Media 7/2010 from a twofold perspective: as a right for audiences (Article 4, paragraphs 5 and 6) which shall be fulfilled by operators, and as a right for operators for their editorial policies not to be interfered (Article 10). Regarding the first perspective, this right of audiences to receive diverse audiovisual media is specified in Article 4.5: 'All individuals are entitled to informative communication being conducted in compliance with the duty of care in terms of verification of the truthfulness of information and for communication to be respectful toward political, social and cultural diversity.' The next paragraph (Article 4.6) complements this right: 'All individuals are entitled to be informed of events of general interest and to receive information and opinion in a clearly separated manner.'

220. The right for operators to editorial freedom is included in Article 10 where freedom in rendering audiovisual media services is acknowledged. '1. Audiovisual media service providers are entitled to establish their editorial policy by selecting the contents and determining broadcasting times.'

§2. Fair Representation in Election Periods

221. The act that governs election advertising is Organic Act 5/1985, on the General Electoral System (Articles 58 and 60–68), complemented by two other regulations:

- Organic Act 10/1991, on Electoral Advertising in Radio Broadcasting Municipal Stations.
- Organic Act 14/1995, on Electoral Advertising in Local Terrestrial Television.

222. The principles comprised in the range of measures on this kind of advertising are summarized as follows:

(a) To avoid discrimination against any political party in public media; as a result, political parties are assigned advertising spaces as per their results in former elections and, for parties that run for the first time, as per their presence in electoral districts.
(b) The right to contract electoral advertising in print media, on municipal radio stations and on private local television stations is established.
(c) A specific right of rectification during the election period is regulated.
(d) Special attention is given to the publication of results of electoral surveys (Article 69).

§3. News and Current Affairs Programmes

223. There is no specific regulation of news and current affairs programmes regarding political content. However, there are some restrictions in electoral period. Spain has an Electoral Board (Junta Electoral), a legal-political body that supervises public broadcaster news programmes in order to protect pluralism. According to Organic Act 5/1985, on General Electoral Regime, 'Respect for political and social pluralism, as well as information neutrality in the state-owned media during election periods, shall be guaranteed by the organisation of these media and their control as provided for by law' (Article 65). As there is no specific regulation for political pluralism in Spain beyond generic requirements, the Electoral Board, becomes de facto the main regulating authority of political pluralism in the public media in election periods. It has interpreted that newscasts time should be distributed in weighted blocks in function of the number of votes obtained in the previous equivalent elections (Cf. Almirón, Capurro & Santcovksy (2010)).

§4. Political Advertising

224. Institutional advertising results from the need of public administration, at its different levels, to inform and promote adherence to its activities and proposals. Act 29/2005 on Institutional Advertising and Communication establishes the principle for the Government to not conduct public communication activities favouring any political party: 'Detaching political opinion from true, neutral information on public policy must be a fundamental principle of the Government's communication activity through institutional campaigns. Institutional advertising and communication must service the needs and interest of citizens and facilitate the exercise of their rights as well as promote the fulfilment of their duties, instead of pursuing inadequate goals involving the use of public funds' (Preamble to the Act).

225. It establishes as a requirement for an institutional advertisement or communication campaign that it raises awareness amongst citizens or provides them with information (Article 3). Prohibitions are established too:

> Article 4. 1. 'It shall be prohibited to promote or engage in campaigns:

(a) That aim to highlight the management achievements or goals reached by the government(s).
(b) That openly discredit, hinder or disrupt policies or any action lawfully conducted by another public authority in the exercise of its competencies.
(c) That include messages of a discriminatory or sexist nature or which go against constitutional principles, values and rights.
(d) That directly or indirectly entice violence or behavior contrary to public order.

> 2. Messages or the presentation of institutional advertising or communication campaigns shall not lead to confusion with symbols, ideas, expressions, designs or images used for any political formation or social organisation.

3. Institutional advertising campaigns that fail to be clearly identified as such and which fail to expressly mention the promoting or contracting Administration shall not be broadcast.'

Chapter 5. Advertising Rules

§1. Various Forms of Commercial Communication

226. Article 2 of General Law 7/2010, on Audiovisual Media, contains a series of definitions that describe, in addition to other concepts, the different commercial communication types.

227. First, section 24 provides a definition of 'audiovisual commercial communication', an umbrella term that covers a number of definitions. It is thus defined as 'Images or sounds that are designed to promote, directly or indirectly, the goods, services or image of an individual or body corporate engaged in an economic activity'. Such images or sounds accompany or are included in a programme in return for payment to the service provider.

228. In any case, the following are forms of audiovisual commercial communication: 'television and radio advertisements, sponsorships, teleshopping and product placement'.'

229. Section 25 then defines an advertisement as 'Any form of message from a public or private company or an individual in relation to its commercial, industrial, artisanal or profession activity with a view to promoting the supply of its goods or the provision of its services, including immovable property, rights and obligations.'

230. Section 26 of Article 2 defines teleshopping as 'The audiovisual television communication of direct offers to the public with a view to the supply of goods or provision of services, including immovable property, rights and obligations.'

231. Section 27 of Article 2 then goes on to define telepromotion as 'Audiovisual commercial communication in which the presenter or any of the main individuals involved in a programme describes, through the use of the scenery, setting or props, the features of a product or service for a period that clearly exceeds that of an advertisement, in such a way that the announcement cannot be broadcast separately from the programme in question.'

232. Section 28 defines self-promotion as 'Audiovisual media that provides information on the service provider's scheduling, specific programmes or programme packages, or ancillary products directly relating to these.'

233. Section 29 defines sponsorship as 'Any contribution that a public or private company or individual not engaged in the provision of audiovisual media services or in the production of audiovisual works makes towards the financing of audiovisual media services or programmes with a view to promoting its name, trade mark, image, activities or products.'

234. Section 30 defines cultural sponsorship as 'Any contribution that an institution, company or foundation makes towards the production of audiovisual works, television and radio programmes and/or digital content relating to cultural, social or sports promotion subjects, with a view to promoting its activities, trade mark and/or image or as an expression of its corporate social responsibility.'

235. Section 31 defines product placement as 'Any form of audiovisual commercial communication that involves including, showing or referring to a product, service or trade mark within a programme.'

§2. Restrictions on Content

236. General Law 7/2010, on Audiovisual Media, stipulates in Article 7.3 on the rights of minors that 'commercial communications shall not cause moral or physical harm to minors', and these communications are therefore subject to the following limitations:

(a) They shall not directly encourage minors to buy or hire a product or service by exploiting their inexperience or credulity.
(b) They shall not directly encourage minors to persuade their parents or third parties to purchase the goods or services being advertised.
(c) They shall not exploit the special trust minors place in their parents, teachers or others.
(d) They shall not show minors in dangerous situations without good reason.
(e) They shall not encourage conduct that promotes inequality between men and women.
(f) Commercial communications relating to products that specifically target children, such as toys, shall not be misleading with regard to the product's features or safety or the capacities or skills needed by minors to use the product without causing harm to themselves or third parties.

237. General Law 7/2010, on Audiovisual Media, prohibits commercial communications in any of the following forms:

(1) 'Illicit publicity is advertising that threatens the dignity of the person or violates the values and rights recognised in the Constitution and defined in article 3 of Law 34/1988, on General Advertising. All commercial communication that violates human dignity or encourages discrimination on the grounds of sex, race or ethnic origin, nationality, religion or belief, disability, age or sexual orientation. In addition, all advertising that uses images of women in a degrading or discriminatory manner is also prohibited.
(2) Commercial communication that is surreptitious or uses subliminal techniques is prohibited.
(3) Commercial communication that encourages behaviour that is prejudicial to health is prohibited.
In all cases the following forms are prohibited:

    (a) The commercial communication of cigarettes and other tobacco products, and of the companies that produce them.

(b) The commercial communication of medicines and health products that contravenes the provisions of Article 78, sections 1 and 5, of Law 29/2006, of 26 July, on Guarantees and Rational Use of Medicines and Health Products.
(c) The televised commercial communication of alcoholic beverages containing over 20° of alcohol.
(d) Television commercial communication of alcoholic below 20° when broadcast outside the period between 20:30 and 06:00 on the following day, unless such alcohol advertising forms an indivisible part of the acquisition of rights and the production of the signal to be broadcast.
(e) The commercial communication of beverages containing less than 20% alcohol by volume when it is directed at minors, encourages excessive consumption or associates consumption with improved physical condition, social success or better health.

(4) Commercial communication that encourages environmentally damaging behaviour is prohibited.
(5) Commercial communication that encourages behaviour that is prejudicial to personal safety is prohibited.
(6) Televised commercial communication that is political in nature is prohibited, except in the cases provided for in Organic Law 5/1985, of 19 June, on the General Electoral System.

§3. Time and Frequency Restrictions

238. Restrictions on commercial breaks are reflected in Article 14, which stipulates that audiovisual television media service providers may broadcast twelve minutes of advertisements per clock hour. Radio, related and interactive services are entitled to broadcast advertisements freely.

239. Only advertisements and teleshopping are taken into account when calculating those twelve minutes, and sponsorships and product placement are excluded. Telepromotion is also excluded from the calculation when the duration of the individual telepromotion announcement is clearly longer than an advertisement and when the telepromotion announcement as a whole does not exceed thirty-six minutes a day or three minutes per clock hour. In addition, television advertisements must respect the integrity of the programme in which they are inserted and the parts that comprise it. In particular, the transmission of films made for television (excluding series, serials and documentaries), feature films and television news programmes may be interrupted once in every scheduled thirty-minute period. In the case of children's programmes, interruptions are permitted once in every scheduled, uninterrupted thirty-minute period if the programme lasts for more than thirty minutes. The televised broadcast of sports events may only be interrupted by one-off advertisements in the case of a delay in the event. Advertisements may be inserted in such transmissions, whether or not they contain separate parts, provided that they do not disrupt viewers' experience of the event. Lastly, television advertising and teleshopping may not be inserted during any religious services.

§4. Sponsorship

240. Section 29 of Article 2 of General Law 7/2010, on Audiovisual Media, defines sponsorship as follows: 'Any contribution made by a public or private company or individual not engaged in the provision of audiovisual media services or in the production of audiovisual works towards the financing of audiovisual media services or programmes with a view to promoting its name, trade mark, image, activities or products.'

241. Section 30 defines cultural sponsorship as 'Any contribution that an institution, company or foundation makes towards the production of audiovisual works, television and radio programmes and/or digital content relating to cultural, social or sports promotion subjects, with a view to promoting its activities, trade mark and/or image or as an expression of its corporate social responsibility.'

§5. Product Placement

242. General Law 7/2010, on Audiovisual Media, stipulates that audiovisual media service providers have the right to include, in exchange for economic compensation, product placements in feature films, short films, documentaries, films made for television and series, sports programmes and entertainment programmes. Product placement is prohibited in children's programmes only. Section 31 of Article 2 of General Law 7/2010, on Audiovisual Media, defines the concept of product placement as follows: 'Any form of audiovisual commercial communication that involves including, showing or referring to a product, service or trade mark within a programme.' General Law 7/2010, on Audiovisual Media, distinguishes it from surreptitious audiovisual television commercial communication, defined in section 32 of Article 2 as 'The indirect or direct representation in words or pictures of the goods, services, name, trade mark or activities of a producer of goods or a provider of services in programmes, other than product placement, when such representation is intended by the audiovisual media service provider to serve as advertising and might mislead the public as to its nature. Such representation is considered to be intentional in particular if it is done in return for payment or for similar consideration.'

Chapter 6. Right to Information

§1. Access to Major Events

243. Article 20 of General Law 7/2010, on Audiovisual Media, sets out the power to ban the encoded transmission of events of general interest for society and stipulates that the Market and Competition Commission (CNMC) must draw up, by means of a reasoned decision, a biennial catalogue of events of general interest for society to be broadcast free to air on television with state coverage. This process shall also determine whether these events should be available by whole or partial live coverage or, where necessary on grounds of public interest, whole or partial deferred coverage.

244. The events of general interest for society that may be included in said catalogue should be selected from the following options:

(a) The winter and summer Olympic Games.
(b) Official matches of the Spanish national football and basketball teams.
(c) The semi-finals and finals of the European Football Championship and the Football World Cup.
(d) The final of the UEFA Champions League and Copa del Rey football competitions.
(e) One game per match day of the Spanish First Division Professional Football League, selected by the association responsible for the league at least ten days in advance.
(f) Grand Prix motor racing events held in Spain.
(g) Grand Prix motorcycle events held in Spain.
(h) European and World handball championship matches involving the Spanish national team.
(i) The Vuelta a España bicycle race.
(j) The UCI Road World Championships bicycle race.
(k) Davis Cup tennis matches involving Spain.
(l) Semi-final and final matches of the French Open tennis tournament involving Spanish players.
(m) Spain's participation in the European Aquatics Championships, World Aquatics Championships, World Championships in Athletics and European Athletics Championships.
(n) Major national and international competitions held in Spain that are subsidized by the state or the autonomous communities.

245. Exceptionally, and by a two-thirds majority, the CNMC may include other events in the catalogue if it considers them to be of general interest for society.

246. The CNMC must notify the European Commission of the catalogue and the measures for its implementation.

§2. Short News Reports

247. Article 19.3 of General Law 7/2010, on Audiovisual Media, sets out the right to obtain exclusive broadcasting rights to audiovisual content and stipulates citizens' minimum access to such content. It states the following: 'An exclusive broadcasting right shall not limit citizens' rights to information. Audiovisual media service providers that have obtained exclusive broadcasting rights to an event of general interest for society shall allow other service providers to broadcast short news reports on reasonable, objective and non-discriminatory terms. This service shall be used for general news programmes only and shall be used in on-demand audiovisual media services only if the media service provider itself is offering the same programme by deferred coverage. No compensation shall be payable when a news report about an event, single set of events or sports competition is broadcast as part of a general news bulletin broadcast by deferred coverage and with a duration of less than 90 seconds. This payment exemption does not, however, include the costs required to produce the news report.'

Chapter 7. Access to Networks

§1. Must-Carry Regulations

248. The General Law on Audiovisual Media 7/2010 grants (Articles 11&31) that audiovisual media providers have the right of access to electronic communication services as Telefónica, Vodafone or Orange for the broadcasting of channels and programme catalogues, subject to technical capacity constraints of their network and in accordance with the provisions of sectoral legislation on telecommunications and electronic communications services. They must also guarantee that images and sounds are broadcast in such a way that makes interactivity possible. The terms and conditions of this access shall be freely agreed by the parties involved. However, the General Law on Audiovisual Media introduces some weak must-offer/must-carry obligations in order to ensure that the pluralism of information and audiovisual content is maintained. The public broadcaster, RTVE, shall guarantee the access of their radio and television channels to cable, satellite and Internet protocol (IPTV) television broadcasting service providers without any financial compensation. Private audiovisual media services with national coverage licences shall as well have granted access of their main free-to-air television channels to telecommunications providers, following agreement of the appropriate financial compensation between the parties involved. This is a fundamental change in Spanish legislation, since previously private free-to-air broadcasters had to provide their broadcasts free of charge to cable and satellite platforms. However, this obligation applies only to their main channels and therefore excludes special-interest channels such as Neox, Nova, Divinity, Energy and FDF. Local and regional channels are also excluded from this obligation.

Chapter 8. Standards and Interoperability

249. With respect to conditional access systems and services, Spanish legislation already introduced a set of rules in 2004 (Royal Decree 2296/2004, of 10 December, which establishes the regulations on electronic communication markets, access to networks and numbering). The following conditions must be fulfilled:

(a) Conditional access service operators and providers shall offer digital TV and radio broadcasting service providers, under fair, reasonable and non-discriminatory terms, the technical means to allow the latter to provide users of decoders operated by them with access to their services.
(b) Conditional access service providers shall keep separate financial accounts for the purposes of providing such services.
(c) Owners of conditional access systems shall be required to licence a common interface to manufacturers of consumer equipment, under fair, reasonable and non-discriminatory terms, for the purposes of connecting other conditional access systems.

250. These conditions were set out in Article 24.1 of the General Law 7/2010, on Audiovisual Media, as follows: 'The conditional access systems and services used to access the digital terrestrial television service in conditional access pay mode shall be free-to-air.'

251. DDT audiovisual signals are transmitted using multiplexes that emit several digital channels. It is common for several different television operators to share a single multiplex, and said operators must agree either to manage it themselves or, as tends to be the norm, request that a third party manage it for them.

252. Most national operators transfer management of the multiplex to a third party in the telecommunications sector in order to avoid conflicts. The Market and Competition Commission (CNMC) is the independent regulatory authority responsible for mediating any conflicts that arise. In the event of conflicts, the CNMC intervenes when the channels cannot reach an agreement concerning management of the multiplex, in the absence of a majority, or when, even with a majority, a series of basic principles are not respected that could affect the rights of the outvoted entity within the group. The CNMC considers that, in the event of a lack of agreement concerning management of the multiplex, the contracting process must be carried out in accordance with the principles of transparency and a procedure that allows the interested parties to submit tenders. In addition, the CNMC considers that the tenders submitted must be transparent and non-discriminatory, with price differentiation for the different services offered and without discrimination between concessionaires. Furthermore, in the event that the management company is partly owned by any of the concessionaires, the CNMC shall monitor compliance with the above principles with greater scrutiny and may exercise greater control of tender prices and supervise transfers within the group. Finally, in order to safeguard competition, the CNMC stipulates that the term of the contract signed by the digital multiplex management company and the service provider must not exceed five years.[10]

10. CMT, resolution concerning the conflict between Canal 7 de Televisión, S.A. and Kiss TV Digital, S.L, Televisión Digital Madrid, S.L. and Iniciativas Radiofónicas y de Televisión, S.L, in relation to the choice of digital multiplex manager and carrier support service provider for the local digital television service in Pozuelo de Alarcón, Aranjuez and Collado Villalba.

Part IV. Cross-Ownership Regulations

253. This part will focus solely on the regulations relating to national media concentration, since the seventeen autonomous communities present a wide range of rules and situations. Media ownership was not regulated in Spain until relatively recently: 1987 for radio broadcasters and 1988 for television companies, when the first law relating to private television was enacted (Law 10/1988 on Private Television).

254. Media concentration laws in Spain have traditionally differed from those in other Western countries, since there are no rules to prevent press concentration or media cross-ownership. The reasons for this are historical. Most of the Spanish press played an important and positive role in the country's democratization process, so any control over ownership was considered a form of unlawful state control over freedom of expression. In addition, the financial interests of Spanish press groups in the development of private television in Spain collaborated against the powers that be to impede any attempts to place limits on press and television media cross-ownership. Consequently, the only regulation that existed within Spanish democracy to limit media ownership concentration applied to television and radio.

255. The absence of such media cross-ownership legislation has had a profound effect on the media sector in Spain, because it enabled between five and seven medium-sized multimedia groups to emerge in the pre-crisis era that competed against each other in the television, radio, press and Internet sectors. Therefore, the media sector in Spain appeared to be relatively diverse in monomedia terms, but it had a high degree of media cross-ownership until 2012. However, the economic downturn sparked a wave of consolidation across the media industries, and this led to a reduction in media diversity between 2010 and 2014, especially in the television broadcasting and radio sector.

256. The most profound reform of Spanish media concentration regulations since 1989 has been brought about, to a great extent, by the digital television transition process. It was impossible to retain the limits on shares and licences with the sheer number of digital channels that were emerging. The socialist government therefore issued Royal Decree Law 1/2009, of 24 February, on Urgent Telecommunications Measures, which amended Law 10/1988 on Private Television and included new rules regarding broadcasting ownership. The entire new regulation concerning media ownership concentration was finally incorporated into the General Law on Audiovisual Media that was approved in April 2010. The biggest change was the introduction of a limit on the audience share of each operator in the event of a merger in order to prevent dangerous ownership concentration. However, several limitations on licence ownership are still in place. The new regulation retained the principle whereby an individual or body corporate directly or indirectly holding 5% or more of the share capital or voting rights of a broadcasting licence holder cannot have significant holdings in any other company within the same area of coverage. There is, however, an important exception for national broadcasting licence holders, which may simultaneously hold shares in several national television stations as the result of a merger, provided that they have no more than 27% of the total audience during the twelve consecutive months prior to the acquisition. This percentage was carefully chosen with the sole purpose of preventing a merger between the two dominant commercial channels in Spain, Telecinco and Antena 3 TV, which are owned by Mediaset and A3 Media groups, respectively.

257. To safeguard external pluralism, the regulation states that no individual or body corporate that, directly or indirectly, owns or has voting rights in a national broadcasting licence holder may acquire a significant holding or voting rights of another broadcasting licence holder, where such an acquisition would prevent the existence of at least three national broadcasting licence holders. A minimum threshold of three independent operators was therefore established. The new regulation also restricts the number of DTT multiplexes that can be owned by a single operator, as a safeguard for the future. It stated that no individual or body corporate could acquire significant holdings or voting rights in a broadcasting licence holder if this involved controlling more than two public multiplexes, out of the six national digital commercial multiplexes that existed in 2010. Again, a minimum threshold was established of three multiplex operators in the market.

258. The General Law on Audiovisual Media also regulates ownership in the radio industry. It states that an individual or body corporate may control up to 50% of the radio broadcasting licences available in a certain area, provided that the total number of overlapping radio broadcasting licences controlled in that area is no higher than five. An individual can also control up to a third of the radio broadcasting licences with total or partial state coverage. Where there is only one frequency available in an area, no individual or body corporate may control more than 40% of such radio broadcasting licences in the same region or autonomous community. These percentages do not take public radio stations into account, and the limits apply separately to analogue and digital radio stations. These limits are established in line with the market status quo, which is dominated by frequencies owned by the radio group PRISA Radio (formerly Unión Radio).

259. With regard to local terrestrial television, Law 41/1995, of 27 December, on Local Terrestrial Television, which was amended in 2002 and 2003, states that broadcasting licence holders may not create a network or enter into network agreements with other licence holders. They may do so only after receiving authorization from the government of the region in which they are located.

Part V. Supervision: Media Regulators

260. Until 2013, Spain was the only European country without a nationwide independent regulatory authority for the audiovisual industry. Broadcasting matters were initially monitored by a low-level department at the Ministry of Industry. Later, a new independent audiovisual regulatory body was defined by the General Law on Audiovisual Media in 2010. However, political disagreements prevented its development and enactment as an official body. Finally, the People's Party decided to merge the existing regulatory bodies in the fields of telecommunications, energy and competition and created the Market and Competition Commission ('Comisión Nacional de los Mercados y de la Competencia', CNMC) in 2013. This body was granted some powers relating to audiovisual matters, especially with regard to content and advertising limits, but none relating to licensing or media ownership concentration control, which remains in the hands of the government. The government justified this new independent cross-sectoral body by stating that it was a cost-cutting measure. The CNMC should be independent; however, the government appoints all ten of its members for a six-year period and parliament alone has the power to veto such appointments.

261. The CNMC is a 'super-regulator', since it encompasses a number of different economic sectors and areas of interest. As a result, no single independent authority deals solely with media-related issues. The fact that media regulation and general market competition are combined may hinder the development of clear, specific policies concerning freedom of expression and media pluralism. No specific relationship is provided for between the media and competition either in the regulations or within the CNMC. The specific characteristics of media markets are therefore not taken into account. This issue was raised by the Spanish Supreme Court, which, in its reference for a preliminary ruling, asked the Court of Justice of the EU whether 'this super-regulator' introduced by the new CNMC law could be regarded as compatible with EU law, since it could threaten its independence (Case C-424/15, Judgement of the Court, 19.10.2016, *Ormaetxea Garai and Lorenzo Almendros v. Administración del Estado*).

Chapter 1. Organization

262. The CNMC exercises its functions through two governing bodies: the Board and the Chairperson, who is also the Chairperson of the Board. The Board is the collective decision-making body. It is made up of ten members who are appointed by the government, following a proposal from the Ministry of Finance and Competitiveness, from individuals with recognized standing and professional experience in the Commission's area of action, following their appearance before the corresponding commission of the Congress of Deputies. The term of office is six non-renewable years and is subject to a strict code of incompatibilities. The Board may meet in plenary session or in a chamber. To this end, it is organized into two chambers: one dedicated to competition issues (Competition Chamber) and the other to supervision of regulated sectors (Regulatory Supervision Chamber). The plenary is made up of all members of the Board and is presided over by the Chairperson. In addition, the CNMC has four directorates (Competition; Energy; Telecommunications and the Audiovisual Industry; and Transport and the Postal Sector).

Chapter 2. Tasks

263. The CNMC's main function is to enforce Spanish and EU antitrust legislation, with a particular focus on anti-competitive practices, control of concentrations and public aid control. It also promotes competition through studies, research projects and industry reports, and market unity. It resolves conflicts between economic operators and supervises and controls all economic sectors, with particular attention to the gas and electricity, electronic communications, audiovisual, railway and airport and postal service markets.

264. The CNMC's functions with regard to the audiovisual industry fall far short of the initial concept of an independent regulatory agency for the audiovisual industry set out in General Law 7/2010, on Audiovisual Media. The government controls public and private radio and television at state level through the Ministry of Industry (licences) and the Ministry of the Presidency (catalogue of events of general interest), and leaves little scope of action to the CNMC, which is responsible for monitoring European quotas, the proper announcement of TV schedules, protection of minors, advertising self-regulation, exclusive broadcasts, fulfilment of the public service mission, free movement of European audiovisual broadcasts and other minor issues. According to Article 9 of Law 3/2013, of 4 June, on the Creation of the Market and Competition Commission, its functions in the audiovisual market are as follows:

(1) To monitor compliance of providers of state-level television media services, and other providers covered by the legislation, with the obligations concerning the annual broadcast of European works and the pre-financing of the production of such works under the terms established in Article 5 of General Law 7/2010, on Audiovisual Media.
(2) To monitor compliance with the obligations imposed in order to ensure transparency in audiovisual media, television scheduling information and the identification of the service provider.
(3) To monitor compliance with the obligations imposed in order to enforce the rights of minors and people with disabilities in accordance with the provisions of articles 7 and 8 of General Law 7/2010 of 31 March.
(4) To ensure that audiovisual content complies with current regulations and self-regulation codes under the terms established in Article 9 of General Law 7/2010 of 31 March.
(5) To oversee compliance with self-regulation codes on audiovisual content and verify compliance with current regulations under the terms established in Article 12 of General Law 7/2010 of 31 March.
(6) To monitor compliance with the obligations, prohibitions and limits imposed on the exercise of the right to carry out audiovisual commercial communications set out in articles 13 to 18 of General Law 7/2010 of 31 March.
(7) To monitor compliance with the obligations and limits imposed on the exclusive acquisition of audiovisual content, the broadcasting of content included in the catalogue of events of general interest and the sale of exclusive rights to regular Spanish football competitions.

(8) To monitor compliance with the public service mission entrusted to state-level public audiovisual media service providers.

(9) To ensure freedom of reception in Spanish territory of audiovisual services whose owners are established in a member state of the European Union.

(10) To adopt measures to safeguard Spanish legislation when the provider of a television audiovisual media service established in another member state of the European Union directs its service wholly or mainly to the Spanish territory and has established itself in that member state to circumvent the more stringent Spanish rules, in accordance with the procedure set forth in Article 39 of General Law 7/2010 of 31 March.

(11) To make decisions concerning the non-advertising nature of public service or charitable announcements, at the request of the interested parties, in accordance with additional provision 7 of General Law 7/2010 of 31 March.

Chapter 3. Sanctioning Powers

265. The sanctions that may be imposed by the CNMC and the Ministry of Industry within the audiovisual industry are classified into three levels in General Law 7/2010 on Audiovisual Media: very serious, serious and minor infringements. The following are regarded as very serious infringements:

(1) Broadcasting of content that manifestly promotes hatred, contempt or discrimination on the grounds of birth, race, sex, religion, nationality, opinion or any other personal or social circumstances.
(2) Broadcasting of commercial communications that violate human dignity or use images of women in a degrading or discriminatory manner.
(3) The failure to comply with more than 10% of the obligations to reserve an annual percentage of broadcasting time for European works and to pre-finance the European production of motion pictures, films and series made for television, documentaries and animated films and series.
(4) Broadcasting of names, images or any other information that may identify minors in the context of crimes or in broadcasts that discuss their guardianship or parentage.
(5) Commission of the serious infringement set out in Article 58.6 twice in one day on a single audiovisual media channel.
(6) Provision of an audiovisual media service without the relevant licence or without fulfilment of the obligation to give prior notice.
(7) Unauthorized alteration of any of the technical broadcasting parameters set out in the licence for private use of the radio spectrum.
(8) Provision of an audiovisual media service based on an invalid prior notification.
(9) Provision of an audiovisual media service based on an application whose holder has had his or her licence revoked in the last two years in Spain or in a Member State of the European Economic Area.
(10) Failure to comply three times in six months with the basic licence conditions set out in Article 24 of this Law.
(11) Failure to comply with the registration obligation provided for in this Law or the provision of false information to the register.
(12) Conclusion of legal transactions to transfer or lease a service provision licence without fulfilment of the requirements laid down in Article 29.
(13) Failure to comply with decisions adopted by the competent audiovisual authority to restore pluralism in the audiovisual market.
(14) The commitment of four serious infringements in one calendar year.

266. The following are regarded as serious infringements:

(1) Failure to comply with the duty of full identification.
(2) Infringement on more than three days in ten consecutive days of the obligation set out in Article 6.2 to give three-day' notice of a television channel's schedule in an electronic guide.

(3) Infringement of the prohibition on and, as applicable, the conditions for broadcasting content that may be harmful to minors.
(4) Failure to comply with the accessibility requirements on a channel for more than five days in ten consecutive days.
(5) Failure to comply with the instructions and decisions of the audiovisual authority.
(6) Failure to comply with the time limit on advertising and teleshopping where this exceeds the permitted amount by 20%.
(7) Failure to comply with the rest of the conditions provided for in this Law concerning implementation of the various forms of commercial communication set out.
(8) Broadcasting of surreptitious commercial communications that use subliminal techniques that encourage behaviour prejudicial to health under the terms established in Article 18.3, that encourage environmentally damaging behaviour or behaviour prejudicial to personal safety, that are political in nature, except where permitted by law, or that infringe the prohibitions established in the regulations concerning advertising.
(9) Failure to comply with the duty to allow other providers to broadcast short news reports under the terms established.
(10) Failure to comply with the obligations concerning free-to-air broadcasting and the sale of broadcasting rights for the events of general interest for society that are established.
(11) Refusal, resistance or obstruction that prevents, hinders or delays the competent authority's exercise of inspection powers.
(12) Failure to comply with the self-regulation codes of conduct set out in Article 12 of this Law.
(13) Accumulation of four minor infringements in one calendar year.

267. The following are regarded as minor infringements:

(1) Failure to comply with the duty to respond to a request for information from the competent authority or the unjustifiable delay of a response that is required in accordance with this Law.
(2) Failure to comply with the rest of the duties and obligations laid down in this Law that are not defined as serious or very serious infringements.
(3) Failure to comply with non-essential licence conditions.

268. With respect to sanctions, Article 60 states that very serious infringements shall be penalized as follows:

(a) With a fine of between €500,001 and €1,000,000 for television audiovisual media services and between €100,001 and €200,000 for radio audiovisual media services, electronic media service providers and programme catalogue service providers.
(b) They may also be sanctioned by revocation of their licence to provide the audiovisual media service by means of terrestrial airwaves, thereby resulting in termination of the service, in the following cases:

(a) Where the provider has committed the very serious infringement laid down in Article 57.13.
(b) Where the provider has been sanctioned, through a final administrative decision, for committing the very serious infringements laid down in sections 3, 9 and 12 of Article 57 on at least three occasions in a period of not more than two years.
(c) Under no circumstances shall providers of the public audiovisual service be required to cease their activity, given that they are service providers, not licensees, although committing any of the infringements set out in this paragraph shall constitute grounds for dismissal of those in charge and may lead to a complaint by the competent audiovisual authority to the relevant bodies.

(c) They may also be sanctioned with cessation of the effects of the prior notification and therefore cessation of the provision of the audiovisual media service in the following cases:

(a) Where the provider has committed the very serious infringement set out in Article 57.13.
(b) Where the provider has committed the very serious infringement laid down in Article 57.3 on at least three occasions in a period of not more than two years.
(c) Under no circumstances shall providers of the public audiovisual service be required to cease their activity, given that they are service providers, not licensees, although committing any of the infringements set out in this paragraph shall constitute grounds for dismissal of those in charge and may lead to a complaint by the competent audiovisual authority to the relevant bodies.

In both cases above, (b) and (c), public sector operators are safe from the possibility of revocation of licenses or cessation of the provision of the audiovisual service, thanks to the provision that, under no circumstances, shall providers of the public audiovisual service be required to cease their activity, given that they are service providers, not licensees.

(d) In the case of the infringements laid down in sections 6, 7 and 8 of Article 57, in addition to the fine, broadcasts shall be ceased, and the equipment and installations used for broadcasting shall be provisionally sealed.

269. Article 60 states that minor infringements shall be sanctioned with a fine of up to EUR 100,000 for television media services and up to EUR 50,000 for radio audiovisual media services, electronic media service providers and programme catalogue service providers.

Selected Bibliography

Agustín Macías, *Legislación audiovisual y publicitaria* (Ratio Legis, 2011).

Alejandro Rosas, *¿Derecho de rectificación, derecho de respuesta o derecho de réplica?,* 18, Derecho Comparado de la Información, 67, 102 (2011).

Alfonso Morales, *La Transformación de RTVE desde la VIII Legislatura*, (Universitat Autònoma de Barcelona, 2013).

Alfonso Sánchez-Tabernero, *Los grupos de comunicación en España: estrategias frente a la crisis* in Francisco Campos *El cambio mediático,* 59-74, (Comunicación Social, 2010).

Alfonso Vara, *Modelos de pago en el sector de la prensa: una estrategia defensiva* in AEDE, *Libro Blanco de la Prensa Diaria,* 407, 422, (AEDE, 2012).

Ana Azurmendi & Iker Huarte (Eds.), *Retos de Futuro de la Televisión Autonómica. Estructura, Financiación, Contenido y Audiencia* (Servicio Publicaciones Universidad de Navarra, 2016).

Ana Azurmendi, *Derecho de la Comunicación. Guía jurídica para profesionales de los medios,* (Eunsa, 2016).

Ana Azurmendi, *El derecho a la propia imagen* (Civitas, 1997).

Ana Azurmendi, *La despenalización de las intromisiones en los derechos al honor, a la intimidad personal y a la propia imagen* in Ernesto Villanueva (coord.) *Derecho de la Información, culturas y Sistemas jurídicos comparados,* 313, 335, (Instituto de Investigaciones jurídicas de la UNAM, 2007).

Ana Azurmendi, *Reforms to the European regional minority-language television corporations in the current context of crisis,* 68 Revista Latina CS, 355, 382 (2013).

Ángel García, *Régimen jurídico y mercado de la televisión de pago España,* (UOC, 2012).

Ángel García, *Régimen jurídico y mercado de la televisión en abierto en España,* (UOC, 2012).

Antoni Rubí, *Publicidad y libertad de expresión* (Thompson-Civitas, 2008).

Carles Llorens, Helena P. Grau & Virginia Luzón, *Mapping Digital Media – Spain.* https://www.opensocietyfoundations.org/sites/default/files/mapping-digital-media-spain-20131023.pdf (accessed 12 January 2018).

Carles Llorens. *Spain's Media Concentration Policy: A Patchwork Crucial to the Understanding of the Spanish Media System.* 4 International Journal of Communication 4, 844, 864 (2010).

Carles Vendrell, *El Mercado de los derechos de imagen,* (Thomson-Reuters, Aranzadi, 2014).

Carlos Lema, *La publicidad comparativa en la Unión Europea,* 291, Revista de Derecho Mercantil, 313, 326, (2014).

Carlos Lema, *Problemas jurídicos de la publicidad,* (Marcial Pons, 2007).

Carolina Pina y Cristina Mesa, *El derecho a la comunicación comercial,* in M. Carmen Chinchilla & Miguel Azpitarte, *Estudios sobre la Ley general de la comunicación audiovisual,* 255, 311. (Aranzadi, 2011).

Celia Martínez, *Derecho de la publicidad.* (Aranzadi, 2015).

Elisabet Malaret & Marta Timón, *Las competencias de la Comisión Nacional de los Mercados y la Competencia en el sector audiovisual* in Matilde Carlón, *La Comisión Nacional de los Mercados y la Competencia,* 445, 507 (Aranzadi, 2014).

Emili Prado, *Televisión e Internet* in Enrique Bustamante (coord.) *Las industrias culturales audiovisuales e Internet,* 45, 56 (Ideco, 2010).

Emilio Guichot, *Derecho de la Comunicación,* (3rd ed., Iustel, 2015).

Emilio J. Lázaro (Coord.), *Comentario a la Ley General de Publicidad* (Thompson-Reuters, 2009).

Emilio J. Lázaro, *Derecho de la publicidad,* (Thomson Reuters, 2012).

Enrique Bustamante, Rafael Díaz et al., *España 2015: Diagnóstico del Servicio Público de Radio, Televisión y Servicios Interactivos. Propuestas para una ciudadanía democrática,* http://eprints.ucm.es/33638/ (accessed 12 January 2018).

Francesc Trillas & Ramon Xifre, *Institutional reforms to integrate regulation and competition policy: Economic analysis, international perspectives, and the case of the CNMC in Spain,* 40 Util. Policy 75, 87 (2016).

Francisco CAMPOS, *Los nuevos modelos de gestión de las empresas mediáticas, 16* Estudios sobre el Mensaje Periodístico, 13, 30, (2010).

Gema Alcolea & M. Estrella Gutiérrez, *El Sector Televisivo Español en el Contexto de Crisis Económica: Análisis y Perspectivas Jurídico-Empresariales.* 6 Re-Presentaciones Period. 6, 125, 144 (2010).

Igancio Bel y Loreto Corredoira (dirs.), *Derecho de la Información. El ejercicio del derecho a la información y su jurisprudencia* (Centro de Estudios Constitucionales, 2015).

Javier Marzal, Jessica Izquierdo & Andrés Casero, *La crisis de la televisión pública* (Aldea Global, 2015)

Joan Balcells & Agustí Cerrillo et al., *Internet, Derecho y Política. Una década de transformaciones* (UOC & Huygens, 2014).

José J. Quirós & Leticia Cabrera, *Ética y Derecho en la publicidad.* (Comares, 2013).

José Mª García, *Los grupos multimedia españoles. Análisis y estrategias* (UOC, 2016).

José Mª García, M. José Serrano & Gema Alcolea, *New Televisión Platforms in Spain and Their Influence on the Market,* 69, Revista Latina CS, 390, 417, (2014).

Selected Bibliography

José R. De Verda (Coord.) *Derecho al honor. Tutela constitucional, Responsabilidad civil y otras cuestiones* (Aranzadi, 2013).

Juan Carlos de MIGUEL& Miguel A. Casado (Coord), *Televisiones autonómicas. Evolución y crisis del modelo público de proximidad* (Gedisa, 2012).

Juan M. Martínez. *La protección jurídica de los menores en el entorno audiovisual.* (Thompson Reuters-Aranzadi, 2013).

Juan P. Artero. *El mercado de la televisión en España: oligopolio,* (Ediciones Deusto, 2008)

Juan Pablo Artero & Alfonso Sánchez-Tabernero, *Media and Telecommunications Concentration in Spain (1984-2012),* 30 European Journal of Communication, 319–336 (2015).

Judith Clares Miguel A. Casado et al., *Políticas culturales y de comunicación. La intervención pública en cine, televisión y prensa.* (UOC, 2013).

Karen Arriaza, *The Situation of National and Regional Public Television in Spain Public Media in the Crossroad,* 34 Nordicom Review 145, 156 (2013).

Loreto Correidora & Lorenzo Cotino (dirs.), *Libertad de expresión e información en Internet. Amenazas y protección de los derechos personales,* (Centro de Estudios Políticos y Constitucionales, 2013).

Luis A. Cucarella, *Rectificación, Tribunales y Medios de Comunicación* (La Ley, 2008).

M. Carmen Chinchilla & Miguel Azpitarte. *Estudios sobre la Ley general de la comunicación audiovisual.* (Aranzadi, 2011).

María A. Moretón, *El Secreto profesional de los periodistas. De deber ético a derecho fundamental* (Centro de Estudios Políticos y Constitucionales, 2012).

María A. Moretón, *El Secreto profesional de los periodistas: Configuración jurídica* in Ignacio Bel & Loreto Corredoira (dirs.), *Derecho de la Información. El ejercicio del derecho a la información y su jurisprudencia,* 577, 602 (Centro de Estudios Constitucionales, 2015).

María E. Bodas, *La defensa 'post mortem' de los derechos de la personalidad* (Bosch, 2007).

María V. Caruso, *El delito de calumnias y la protección del honor,* (Difusión jurídica, 2008).

Maribel Fernández & Ana Fernández, *Internal Pluralism in the Governance of Public Service Broadcasters in Spain and the Role of Social Groups and Professionals: The Case of RTVE,* 25, Communication & Society, 203, 230 (2012).

Maribel Fernández, *Independent Audiovisual Regulators in Spain: A Unique Case in Europe,* 10, 18, International Journal of Communication, 359, 376, (2007).

Miguel Carvajal & José Alberto García, *From Newspapers to Multimedia Groups. Business Growth Strategies of the Regional Press in Spain,* 2, 3 Journalism Practice, 453, 462, (2008).

Selected Bibliography

Montse Bonet & Josep A. Guimerà, *When efficiency meets clientelism: Spectrum management policy and broadcasting model – The Spanish case*. 31 European Journal of Communication, 411, 425 (2016).

Núria Almirón, *Grupos privados propietarios de medios de comunicación en España: principales datos estructurales y financieros*, 22 (1) Communication & Society, 243, 273 (2009).

Núria Almirón, María Capurro & Pablo Santcovsky, *Electoral Blocks in the Public Media in Spain: An Exception inn Europe*. 34 Quaderns del CAC, 93, 100 (2010).

Pedro Grimalt, *La protección civil de los derechos al honor, a la intimidad y a la propia imagen* (Iustel, 2007).

Pilar Cousido, *Derecho a la Información e Información Pública. Los Secretos Oficiales* in Ignacio Bel & Loreto Correidora (dirs.), *Derecho de la Información. El ejercicio del derecho a la información y su jurisprudencia*, 431, 450, (Centro de Estudios Constitucionales, 2015).

Rafael Díaz, *La relación laborar informativa. La cláusula de conciencia* in Ignacio Bel y Loreto Corredoira (dirs.), *Derecho de la Información. El ejercicio del derecho a la información y su jurisprudencia*, 327, 345 (Centro de Estudios Constitucionales, 2015).

Reuters Institute for the Study of Journalism, *Reuters Institute Digital News Report 2017*, (Oxford, 2017).

Ricard Martínez, *Una aproximación crítica a la autodeterminación informativa*, (Thompson-Civitas, 2004).

Rodrigo Bercovitz y Juan J. Marín, *El límite de la copia privada y las redes de intercambio peer to peer*, 20 Revista Aranzadi de derecho de deporte y entretenimiento 147, 235 (2007).

Samuel D. Warren & Louis D. Brandeis, *The Right to Privacy*, 4, 5, Harvard Law Review 193, 219, (1890).

Santiago Muñoz (dir.), *Derecho de la regulación económica*, vol. 5, 11, 118 (Iustel, 2012).

Sara Medina, *El servicio público de la comunicación audiovisual* in Carmen Chinchilla & Miguel Azpitarte, *Estudios sobre la Ley General de la Comunicación Audiovisual*, 463, 489 (Aranzadi, 2011).

Stephen Barnett, *The Right to One's Own Image: Publicity and Privacy Rights in the United States and Spain*. 47 AJCL, 555, 581 (1999).

Tomás de la Quadra, *La Ley 7/2010, de 31 de Marzo, General de la Comunicación Audiovisual: del servicio público a la liberalización en un sistema dual* in M. Carmen Chinchilla & Miguel Azpitarte, *Estudios sobre la Ley general de la comunicación audiovisual*, 26, 69. (Aranzadi, 2011).

William Prosser, *Privacy*, 48, California Law Review, 383 (1960).

Selected Bibliography

Xavier Seuba, *Derechos fundamentales y observancia de propiedad intelectual* in Joan Balcells, Agustí Cerrillo et al., *Internet, derecho y política una década de transformaciones*, 25, 39, (UOC & Huygens, 2014).

Legislation

Ley 17/2006, de 5 de junio, de la radio y la televisión de titularidad estatal. Boletín Oficial del Estado, 134, (6 June 2006).

Ley 10/1988, de 3 de mayo, de Televisión Privada. Boletín Oficial del Estado, 108, (Th May 1988).

Constitución Española. Boletín Oficial del Estado, (29 December 1978).

Ley 7/2010, de 31 de marzo, General de la Comunicación Audiovisual. Boletín Oficial del Estado, 30157, 30209 (2010).

Ley 6/2012, de 1 de agosto, de modificación de la Ley 7/2010, de 31 de marzo, General de la Comunicación Audiovisual, para flexibilizar los modos de gestión de los servicios públicos de comunicación audiovisual autonómicos. Boletín Oficial del Estado, 184, (2 August 2012).

Ley 3/2013, de 4 de junio, de creación de la Comisión Nacional de los Mercados y la Competencia. Boletín Oficial del Estado, 134, (5 June 2013).

Selected Bibliography

Index

The numbers here refer to paragraph numbers.

Index

Made in the USA
Monee, IL
22 October 2026

66389951R00070